LOVE THAT LASTS

Sep 2010
To: Kristi,
From: Sharo

LOVE
that
LASTS

JILL BRISCOE

TYNDALE HOUSE PUBLISHERS, INC. WHEATON, ILLINOIS

Visit Tyndale's exciting Web site at www.tyndale.com

Love That Lasts

Copyright © 2002 by Jill Briscoe. All rights reserved.

Cover illustration copyright © 2002 by Deborah Hanley. All rights reserved.

Designed by Jenny Swanson

Edited by Linda K. Taylor and Susan Taylor

Published in association with the literary agency of Alive Communications, Inc., 7680 Goddard Street, Suite 200, Colorado Springs, CO 80920.

Scripture quotations marked NLT are taken from the *Holy Bible*, New Living Translation, copyright © 1996. Used by permission of Tyndale House Publishers, Inc., Wheaton, Illinois 60189. All rights reserved.

Scripture quotations marked NIV are taken from the *Holy Bible*, New International Version®. NIV®. Copyright © 1973, 1978, 1984 by International Bible Society. Used by permission of Zondervan Publishing House. All rights reserved.

Scripture quotations marked KJV are taken from the *Holy Bible*, King James Version.

Scripture quotations marked "NKJV" are taken from the New King James Version. Copyright © 1979, 1980, 1982 by Thomas Nelson, Inc. Used by permission. All rights reserved.

Scripture verses marked Phillips are taken from *The New Testament in Modern English* by J. B. Phillips, copyright © J. B. Phillips, 1958, 1959, 1960, 1972. All rights reserved.

Scripture quotations marked *The Message* are taken from *The Message.* Copyright © 1993, 1994, 1996 by Eugene H. Peterson. Used by permission of NavPress Publishing Group. All rights reserved.

Library of Congress Cataloging-in-Publication Data

Briscoe, Jill.
    Love that lasts / Jill Briscoe.
        p. cm.
Includes bibliographical references.
    ISBN 0-8423-5309-7 (pbk.)
    1. Love—Religious aspects—Christianity.   I. Title.
    BV4639 .B818 2002
    241'.4—dc21   2002006526

Printed in the United States of America

08   07   06   05   04   03   02
7   6   5   4   3   2   1

To Stuart,
the love of my life,
who through the gift of grace
has loved me fully, faithfully, and wonderfully
for nearly five decades of adventure,
privilege, and joy in serving Jesus.

Loving those who don't deserve it,
Loving those I hate,
Loving on when all seems lost and loving is too late.
Loving when love's not returned
And when my heart's in pain,
Finding courage deep within to live and love again.

Loving God with all my heart
And enemies as friends,
Loving those who're difficult,
Yet loving till the end.
Finding all-sufficient love when love is hard to find,
Loving and forgiving those who're thoughtless and unkind.

Love like this is gifting from the God who came to give
Life and love through Jesus Christ,
Who died that we might live.
You cannot love without him
In the many ways you should,
Loving unloving people—the bad as well as good.

So put yourself in silence,
And receive the Spirit's power
To love and love without an end until the final hour.
Our human love is not enough
To love a broken race
Into the loving arms of God with tears upon his face.

So love me into loving, Lord,
Reduce me, Lord, to size
Till Jesus, all is Jesus, and you alone the prize.
Work in me by your Spirit till
You melt this heart of stone,
Perfect your work till I at last am loving you alone!
                                        —Jill Briscoe

CONTENTS

INTRODUCTION

❦

Love . . . can outlast anything.
1 CORINTHIANS 13:7 (PHILLIPS)

EVERYONE WANTS TO BE LOVED—THAT'S A GIVEN. BUT
not everyone is loved—that's a fact. Do you know how to give and
receive love? Do you know what real love is, how love behaves, and
where love is to be found? Have you experienced what love feels
like, how it works, and how it can last?

How is your love life? As you look around at your relationships,
which of them could be described as really "loving"? Do you know
how to express love, protect love, offer love, and love on to the end?

As you have probably guessed, this book is all about love. Love that
works and love that lasts. This book is about God's love for us and our
love for God. It's about love for friend and neighbor (no matter how
obnoxious) and love for relative and family (no matter how difficult).
It's about love for employer or employee, love for a loved one, and love
for a hated one. It's even about love for your in-laws!

But it is not only about how to give love; it is about how to allow
yourself to receive love when you have been horribly hurt, rejected,
or abused.

NO SAFE INVESTMENT

C. S. Lewis said,

> There is no safe investment. To love at all is to be vulnera-
> ble. Love anything, and your heart will certainly be wrung
> and possibly be broken. If you want to make sure of keeping

it intact, you must give your heart to no one, not even to an animal . . . avoid all entanglements; lock it up safe in the casket or coffin of your selfishness. But in that casket—safe, dark, motionless, airless—it will change. It will not be broken; it will become unbreakable, impenetrable, irredeemable. . . . The only place outside Heaven where you can be perfectly safe from all the dangers and perturbations of love is Hell. (*The Four Loves* [New York: Harbrace, 1960], 169)

If you have been hurt by love, how can you heal enough to risk having your heart broken all over again? Should you even try? There is, as Lewis said, no safe investment when it comes to love.

Most of us fallen creatures are more interested in getting love than giving love—especially if we have been burned. Yet if we learn to love as we have been created to love, we find it is worth the risk.

A LOVE STORY

Many times love begets love; in other words, we love and that opens the door for others to love us in return.

My father met my mother and fell deeply in love with her. He decided that if he couldn't have my mother by his side forever, he would never marry anyone else. However, she did not respond to his advances and, in fact, rather disliked him.

My father persisted in pursuing her. "Give me a chance," he pled. "If you will go out with me for six months, I will abide by your decision at the end." She reluctantly agreed. So my father got to work, for "love that doesn't work, doesn't work!" He courted my mother with everything he had. He made the investment, not sure that his heart would be intact at the end of the day. He took the risk.

At the end of the six months he had become my mother's constant companion and her best friend. She discovered that she could not live without him. She was irrevocably "in love." He won her to himself through his self-giving love. They married and loved each other for thirty-eight years until his death. I'm so glad my father was willing to have his heart broken or I wouldn't be here writing this book about love that lasts!

Of course, this may not happen to everyone. But even in cases where hope has died and all seems lost, you can still put love's principles and actions into practice. Even if your love elicits no response, you will be a healthier person for having loved. "Love never fails," wrote the apostle Paul in I Corinthians 13:8 (NIV).

That does not mean that love never fails to get a response, but that love never fails to go on loving, whatever the reaction. This sort of love loves on in all circumstances, whether it is reciprocated, rejected, or received. To love others no matter how they respond to you is to love as God loves. After all, God loved a world full of people who hated him—loved them so much that he died for them. This is the greatest love story of all!

As you read this book, my prayer is that you will find the keys to a love that works and lasts, a love that fulfills your life and your dreams in ways beyond your wildest imaginings. Such love was born in Eden, ravaged in the Fall, restored at the Cross, and made available to us when we accept the God who *is* love. He loves us so that we can love others.

Where else would we start to find out about such love but in a well-known and loved Scripture passage: I Corinthians 13. One day Paul wrote about love. He painted a portrait with words, and Jesus sat for it. For in the Lord Jesus Christ we have the perfect picture of the perfect love. Read Paul's words below:

> If I could speak in any language in heaven or on earth but
> didn't love others, I would only be making meaningless
> noise like a loud gong or a clanging cymbal. If I had the gift
> of prophecy, and if I knew all the mysteries of the future
> and knew everything about everything, but didn't love
> others, what good would I be? And if I had the gift of faith
> so that I could speak to a mountain and make it move, with-
> out love I would be no good to anybody. If I gave everything
> I have to the poor and even sacrificed my body, I could

boast about it; but if I didn't love others, I would be of no value whatsoever.

Love is patient and kind. Love is not jealous or boastful or proud or rude. Love does not demand its own way. Love is not irritable, and it keeps no record of when it has been wronged. It is never glad about injustice but rejoices whenever the truth wins out. Love never gives up, never loses faith, is always hopeful, and endures through every circumstance.

Love will last forever, but prophecy and speaking in unknown languages and special knowledge will all disappear. Now we know only a little, and even the gift of prophecy reveals little! But when the end comes, these special gifts will all disappear.

It's like this: When I was a child, I spoke and thought and reasoned as a child does. But when I grew up, I put away childish things. Now we see things imperfectly as in a poor mirror, but then we will see everything with perfect clarity. All that I know now is partial and incomplete, but then I will know everything completely, just as God knows me now.

There are three things that will endure—faith, hope, and love—and the greatest of these is love.

A Prayer before You Start

Jesus, show me love that's giving
me a reason new for living,
finding freedom in forgiving,
help me love again.

Frozen by such cruel rejection,
starved for any real affection,
needing healing and protection,
help me love again.

By your Holy Spirit cheer me,
be thou, Savior, ever near me,
teach me, God, again to fear thee,
help me love again.

—Jill Briscoe

CHAPTER ONE

LOVING GOD BACK

God is love.
1 JOHN 4:8

GOD LOVES US WITH ALL HIS HEART, SOUL, MIND, AND strength, and that is how he wants us to love him back. For this we need Jesus. But for this we have Jesus if we are Christians. Without Jesus we cannot love as God loves. We cannot love him, we cannot love ourselves, and we certainly cannot love others.

God has created us with the capacity to love him fully as he fully loves us. That is why there is this huge need inside our hearts to love and be loved in return. God put it there! Once we find God, we discover how much he loves us, and we find the capacity to truly love others.

There is certainly a longing for intimacy, especially since the infamous horror of September 11, but most people are turning to each other for comfort and fulfillment, and not to God. After the first surge back to church, it's business as usual. People are once again making the elementary mistake of looking first to other people rather than to God to meet the love hunger inside them.

The heart is a "lonely hunter" until it finds God. For this reason there is a universal search for a love that works and lasts, for a love that, as J. B. Phillips puts it, "knows no limit to its endurance, no end to its trust, no fading of its hope; it can outlast anything" (1 Corinthians 13:7).

LOVE IS MORE THAN A WARM PUPPY

I was visiting a Christian campus where I had been invited to speak in chapel. Not everyone who attended that school was a Christian, but the majority were from Christian homes. One night I was invited into the girls dorm for a chat. A group of college kids wanted to talk to me about their favorite subject, and so we were discussing what "real love" is all about.

"Define it for me," I suggested.

"I think love is a warm puppy," someone volunteered.

"Actually," I answered, "love might be a 'wet' puppy, but love is a whole lot more than warm or wet puppies!"

"Love is never having to say you are sorry," someone else added.

"Well," I countered, "only love really knows how to say it's sorry, and that's something all of us need to learn to say many times a day."

"Love is a feeling too big for words," another announced somewhat emotionally.

"But what happens when love doesn't feel like loving anymore? When the feeling that was too big for words shrinks to nothing much at all, we wonder what we saw in the person in the first place. What sort of love is that?" I inquired. We decided that was a big part of the problem. Love doesn't seem to last.

"People move in and out of relationships so easily, according to how they feel," commented Jennifer. "If someone doesn't feel loving anymore, he simply shrugs his shoulders and says things like, 'People change. That's how it is! I didn't plan it this way, but that's the way it goes. Good-bye!'"

She sounded as if she knew what she was talking about.

"My dad just told my mom he didn't love her anymore," a sweet little thing offered. "Took her out to dinner while his friends emptied her stuff onto the front lawn. She couldn't even get into the house when she came back home!"

"That's exactly what my mom did to my dad," added the girl sitting next to her.

"You and I need to talk," said the first. "It sounds like we have a lot in common!"

The girls talked on, feeling secure enough among their peers to share their hurts and their hearts. They spoke not only of their own agony but also that of their parents. They talked with obvious pain of watching dads and moms split up, of the ongoing trauma of court battles that affected them deeply yet excluded them from the process and seemed to have no end.

"I don't want to go home this semester break," offered a pretty girl. "My father moved out after I came to school this spring, and I can't face going back yet. Anyway, where do I go? To my mom's house or my dad's apartment? I don't want to make either of them mad, and I want to support both."

"Wait till you have to go home and meet the three new kids who are living in your house. There they are, sleeping in your bed and wearing the clothes that you left behind, and you are expected to be thrilled about it all! I was told to start calling them my stepbrothers and stepsisters and to move over and make room for them in my life," murmured a sober-looking senior sipping a Coke.

"I'm never going to marry," announced a beautiful redhead. "After watching my parents struggle, I'm scared I would fall out of love too, and I don't want to hurt someone like that."

"Don't you think that's selfish though?" asked a tall sporty-looking girl in a sweat suit. "I still think that love is worth the risk. After all, we can learn by our parents' mistakes and choose right."

"It's not about choosing right," answered another girl. "It's just that people change. It even happens among Christians."

There was a chorus of voices as the girls said that their parents were Christians and they could hardly see the difference between marriages in the church and those out of it. I sat still, absorbing the impact of all of this, realizing the absolute carnage that has taken place in the last twenty years.

DISAPPOINTED BY LOVE

I was listening to the first generation of the new millennium talk about their disillusionment, their severe disappointment with God, life, and love. Most were kids that loved the Lord and loved their parents but were wondering whether it was safe to love anyone else! I thought of the fifteen-year-old I had once met who asked his mother how people who had loved each other so much could hate each other so much—all in one lifetime. This generation is fast becoming as concerned about their parents' heart affairs as they are about their own.

We have succeeded in raising a broken generation, I thought. These young people would face challenges in their relationships we never had to face in our day. What happened to their parents cast a shadow over the way they thought and acted in their own friendships and growing relationships. And it also changed what they believed about what Scripture says about marriage.

As if she had read my thoughts, a sophisticated-looking youngster looked up and said, "Well, they say that by the time we are getting married, marriage to the same spouse for a lifetime will be both unusual and unnecessary! They say we will have different partners for different stages of life. It could make a whole lot of sense," she added somewhat breathlessly. "I mean, you might be a perfect partner for raising kids but not a good companion when your kids are grown and gone. Changing partners isn't all that crazy an idea!"

There was silence for a moment. After all, this was a Christian campus! Any such radical statement should bring some appropriate response, but to my amazement, no response was forthcoming.

"And who are 'they'?" I inquired, breaking the silence.

"The experts," she answered firmly.

"Experts at what?" I asked.

"At knowing what they are talking about. They say that statistics show—"

"But we're not statistics," burst out a cute redhead. "We are people who somehow know that this is not the way things ought to be! When will the people we love best in our lives quit picking and clawing each other to death?"

Now we were getting somewhere!

"What do you think is the way things ought to be?" I asked her gently. "Are there any rules? Is there an 'ought' at all?"

"I don't know anymore," she answered somewhat desperately. "All I know is this mess can't be the way God meant us to treat each other. It can't be!"

"And it isn't," I said firmly, smiling encouragingly at her.

"It isn't?" she asked hopefully.

"It isn't what God had in mind from the first, no." Then we got down to business. "There are many kinds of love, so we should define our terms before we go any further," I began. And this is what I told them.

GOD IS LOVE

The Bible tells us that "God is love" (1 John 4:8, 16). But what sort of love is he made of? Warm fuzzy feelings? Love that quits loving when it is not reciprocated? Is his love conditional—"I'll love you if you love me"? Does he promise to love me only if I'm good, if I don't sleep with my boyfriend or girlfriend before marriage, or if I'm pretty? Does he expect me to say my prayers, go to church, and read my Bible before he will love me back? What *does* the love of God look like? How does it behave? How can I describe it?

The young women listened attentively as I explained that the Greek language has several different words that English translates simply as "love." Those words describe different kinds of love. The word that Paul uses to describe love in 1 Corinthians 13 is *agape.* This word refers to unconditional love. It means that God loves without conditions, irrespective of our reaction or response. It is love "God style," not love American style, or Western style. It is a love that is willing to be rejected and still love on. It is a love that loves the unlovely. It is a love that lays down its life for its friends. Human beings are incapable of loving this way. In order to do this, we need the Holy Spirit in our lives.

Other Greek words describe the kinds of love that we experience. For example, there's *phileo,* which pictures friendship love. And there's *eros,* the "feeling too big for words" sort of love, the love we feel for a boyfriend or girlfriend or spouse. But rarely do we experience agape love.

Imagine what it would be like if we could love others as God loves us. Why, that would revolutionize the world! Yet this is exactly what God requires of us. When we become his children, the Holy Spirit enters our hearts and begins to grow his "fruit," one of which is love—agape love (Galatians 5:22). The Holy Spirit within us then enables us to love God with all our hearts, souls, minds, and strength, and to love our neighbor as much as we love our selfish selves. God does not tell us to do anything that he does not enable us to do! He himself is the enabling of all of his commands.

So how do we respond to this news? How does the love of God get into our hearts in the first place? Well, not without an invitation! "Love has good manners" (I Corinthians 13:5, Phillips). The love of God comes into our hearts when we invite Jesus by his Spirit to come into our lives.

NOT THE WAY THINGS OUGHT TO BE

Let me tell you what happened to me. I was a much-loved child. My father loved me and my mother loved me and my sister loved me, and that was my world. In return, I loved them all back. I was a child of the Second World War, and so I became aware that not everyone loved me. Someone was dropping bombs all over my life in a regular fashion! I was only five years of age when the war broke out. We lived in Liverpool (not a very good idea as the Liverpool docks were a favorite nightly target of the enemy), so I spent many a terrifying night huddled in our air-raid shelter wondering what we had done and why so much hate had been let loose on my happy little head.

When all you have experienced is love at home, it is a puzzle to figure out why there is so much hate afoot outside it. Things were definitely not the way they ought to be! I knew it at that young age, yet no one explained anything to me. My parents were far too busy trying to keep us alive!

So I began to question the character of God. I didn't know what I was doing, but in my little mind I was trying to figure out why, if God was good, he made so many bad people. And if God was big and could do everything, why didn't he stop the war? How big was he anyway? No one was reading my mind, so I drew my own five-year-old conclusions and wondered on. It would be ten more years until I finally got some answers to the puzzles of right and wrong, good and evil, love and hate.

One thing, however, was abundantly clear—things were not the way they ought to be. Somewhere deep inside I knew it. I knew with some strange God-given knowledge that there was a good God with a good plan and it had gone terribly wrong. And I was also sure that somewhere a loving God wanted to put everything right. I knew that he was horrified at the sinfulness of the human race. He wanted to reverse it all until right was triumphing over wrong and love prevailed. Love was the answer! *If all the people in the world would only love each other like my family does,* I thought wistfully, *then what a wonderful world it would be!*

Years later, when a girl called Janet explained that all my internal hopes were right, I could hardly believe my ears! She affirmed all my secret beliefs in the character of God and told me how I could know him for myself. I had been sure deep down inside that he existed, and I had no trouble asking for his help. Janet led me to Christ, and I walked into the arms of a God who loved me and gave his life for me. I heard him say very clearly, *You're right, Jill. Things are not the way they ought to be! First, let me put things right between you and me, and then let's work together to put things right in the hearts of people all over the world.*

LOVING GOD BACK

My heart ached with the joy of it all. God was a God of power, glory, and love. This was his world, and he wanted it back. He wanted to use me in his grand cosmic plan to do my small part! So God forgave me for Christ's sake, and I experienced a love that transcended all the other loves in my life. They paled into insignificance compared to the love I began to know from God and for God. I didn't love my loved ones less; in fact, I actually loved them more. I loved God the most and realized I could never love anyone with that selfless agape love unless I first loved him. He would enrich and enhance all my other loves.

"How did you get him into your life?" asked the girl with the sad eyes, the one who didn't want to go home for the semester break.

I turned to her, reliving my own conversion experience. "I asked Jesus to come into my heart by his Spirit," I replied.

"How did that work?" she asked.

"I said a simple prayer, asking him to forgive my sins and come into my life. I thanked him for dying on the cross for me because I had lived a life that was not what it should have been. I invited him to reverse the trend and direction of my life."

"And did he?" she asked breathlessly.

I answered simply. "If he hadn't, I wouldn't be here!"

There was silence. A silent shadow of love hovered over the room as if the Lord were saying to those sweet young women: "Listen to her, she is telling you the truth. Why don't you come home to me like she did? I'm waiting." And then I invited them to pray with me. Many had made that personal invitation to Christ years ago. A few in the group had not.

For them, I knew life had only just begun—a lifetime of learning what this life of love was all about. Jesus Christ by his Spirit had taken up residence in their hearts, and the possibilities of giving and receiving love—a love that works and lasts—had started. Their lives would take them to the far corners of the world and present new challenges of loving day by daily day. For this they would need Jesus. But from now on, they had Jesus!

I knew that the Bible describes such brand-new converts as newborn babies who need to grow into Christian maturity. My work was cut out for me! I needed to set about a plan to feed them. Babies exhibit "need love." If you don't believe me, hang around a newborn infant who's hungry! Peter told the new Christians to "cry out for this nourishment as a baby cries for milk, now that you have had a taste of the Lord's kindness" (I Peter 2:2-3). My new "babies" were going to need the milk of God's Word.

DISCOVERING GOD'S LOVE

As new converts to Christ begin to read, mark, and inwardly digest the Scriptures, they grow spiritually. Paul uses an analogy for this kind of growth in I Corinthians 13:11. He writes, "When I was a child, I spoke and thought and reasoned as a child does. But when I grew up, I put away childish things." Children act like children, but one day, if things are normal, children become adults and behave like adults. They "put away childish things." In the context of the chapter, Paul means that as believers mature in their faith, they learn how to love as God loves. A baby needs to be loved but does not know how to love in return. But eventually the baby grows up and learns how to give love as well.

Believers need to learn how to love as God loves. They need to move from just being loved to giving love or from "need love" to "gift love." The key lies in the measure of spiritual maturity. The measure of our spiritual maturity lies in our ability to feed on the Word of God and grow up!

"So how do we do that?" asked one of the new believers. "What do you mean, 'Get into the Bible and let the Bible get into you'?"

Well, what *did* I mean? I love the way young people don't let you get away with Christian clichés!

"Well, what I mean is that you buy yourself a Bible if you haven't got one and you begin to read it!" I said.

"Where do we start to read?"

"Try John's Gospel," I suggested.

"Why John's Gospel?"

"Because that's one place you can get to know Jesus. It's an eye-witness account of his life. You can follow him through the pages of the Gospels. You can watch him heal a leper; listen to his sermons and illustrated talks, called parables; follow him to Jerusalem; stand at his cross; visit his tomb; and meet him in the garden like Mary Magdalene did. Yes, start in the Gospels, and learn to love him." This they understood, and away they went to begin to feed on this food we call Scripture.

Of course, I told them that as they learned the behavior God expects of his followers from the Bible, they would need to obey.

"How will we do that?" they inquired.

"Think about what you are reading," I replied. "Whenever you come to a command, underline it in green. Then go out into your day and try to do what it says."

I was on campus for a week, which gave them a chance to report their progress to me. They were soon back saying that they had found a big command in John's Gospel that they didn't have a clue how to obey.

"What is it?" I asked them.

"'I am giving you a new commandment: Love each other,'" they quoted from John 13:34.

"Ah," I said, "you found it!"

"It doesn't seem a fair imperative," objected one of the girls. "You can't command someone to love you."

"It would be fun if you could," laughed her friend.

"If love is only a feeling, you can't," I answered. "You can't command someone to feel love, so don't you see, love must be more than a feeling?"

"Like what?"

"Like actions," I replied.

"Actions without feelings? That sounds cold and sort of—unloving!"

"Well, why don't we study what real love is all about?" I asked them. "I'm here for a few more days, so we could get a start." The small group agreed to meet together and begin this grand adventure. "The place to start, of course, is I Corinthians 13," I said.

"Why?"

"Because in this letter Paul wrote to a lot of unloving people and showed them how things could be different. Paul defines and describes and shows us how love works."

With Bibles in hand we started an investigation into the heady subject of real love. Using the book of I Corinthians as a guide and the Gospels as an illustration of love walking our planet in the person of Jesus Christ, we learned life-changing things that made us people who would never be the same again. I invite you to start this grand adventure too.

LOVING "GOD STYLE"

"God is love," and as we noted above, his love is much more than a nice feeling that may or may not last. So what does this God-style love look like?

First of all, God is three persons—a Trinity. This is very hard for us to fathom because we don't have any concrete analogies for it. The Trinity refers to the three "persons" of God—the Father, the Son, and the Holy Spirit. We can relate to the fact that God is a Father because we all have fathers. The fact that God is a Son is fairly easy to grasp as well. But God is a Spirit? What does that mean? We haven't seen one of those. But what we learn from the Bible about this mysterious and glorious God is that he always existed in three persons and that he is love. These members of the Trinity have always loved each other, forever and ever. We are explicitly told in the Gospels, for example, that God loves his Son.

Twice God's voice is heard from heaven reiterating this fact. At Jesus' baptism by John, a voice from heaven announced, "You are my beloved Son, and I am fully pleased with you" (Luke 3:22). Then again on the Mount of Transfiguration, Peter, James, and John were there to hear that same voice say, "This is my beloved Son" (Matthew 17:5). Jesus was the Father's beloved One, his "One and Only" (John 1:14, NIV).

It follows, then, that the Father loves those who love the Son! Jesus himself said: "The Father himself loves you dearly because you love me" (John 16:27). And in his prayer to his Father about us, Jesus said, "You love them as much as you love me" (John 17:23). That God loves me as much as he loves his Son staggers my mind! Do you believe that God loves you as much as he loves Jesus? That will give you a sense of self-worth in a hurry!

Let me use an illustration to help us understand why God would love those who love his Son.

Years ago our eldest son was leaving for college in Minneapolis. I was to be out of the country with my husband when he went. I couldn't wait to get back and travel up to the Twin Cities to see him and find out how he fared. His sister went with him to help him settle in, and a good friend of ours who lived there met them at the airport. The same friend picked me up for my visit, and I thanked her profusely for all she had done to help Dave. She told me all about it, and then she suddenly said, "Oh, Jill, I do love your son!" Up to that moment she had just been a friend; but as soon as she said that, a warm feeling enveloped me, and I decided she would undoubtedly become one of my closest and best friends in the whole wide world! What made the difference? Her statement of love for my son drew me closer to her than before.

So it is with God. When he looks down from heaven and sees us kneeling in prayer saying, "Father, I love your Son," something happens in his heart. He loves us for it. It gives him special pleasure. Yes, God loves all of us, but he especially loves those who love and respond to his Son.

But God not only loves those who love his Son, God loves those who hate his Son, too. This is what distinguishes agape love from all the other kinds of love. God loves his enemies! We know this to be true because he demonstrated such love for those who were crucifying him: "Father, forgive these people, because they don't know what they are doing" (Luke 23:34).

In fact, without God's love for his enemies, none of us could have been saved! We all were his enemies before we came to repentance and faith in him. "While we were still sinners, Christ died for us" (Romans 5:8, NIV). In fact, "we were restored to friendship with God by the death of his Son while we were still his enemies" (Romans 5:10).

This puts agape love in a class all by itself. This sort of love is unconditional love. It is not a feeling too big for words, and it is a world away from being like a warm puppy! It is love defined in terms of what love does. It is demonstrable love. It is not, "I love you *if.*" It is "I love you *even if.*" It is love that is totally committed to the well-being of the other person, irrespective of the cost to itself. It is love that does the right thing for the beloved even when it doesn't feel like doing it. I assure you that love in the shape of Jesus did not *feel* like hanging on the cross! God-style love is agape love— gift love at its best.

Now the thing that blows us away is the fact that Jesus says to his disciples, "Love your enemies!" (Luke 6:35). For this we need Jesus, but for this we have Jesus!

So God-style love is love that is unconditional. He does not say, "Fulfill the conditions and I will love you" or, "I will love you if you are pretty or if you're good or if you perform acceptably." He says, "I will love you" period!

It was this realization of God's great love to me that broke my heart and drew me to Christ. I had lived eighteen years of my life as his enemy. Some verses of one of my favorite hymns sum it up:

> *God made me for himself to serve him here,*
> *With love's pure service, and in filial fear,*
> *To serve him here, for him to labor now*
> *Then share his Glory where the angels bow.*
>
> *And I poor sinner cast it all away,*
> *Lived for the toil and pleasure of each day.*
> *As if no Christ had shed his precious blood,*
> *As if I owed no homage to my God.*
>
> *Oh, Holy Spirit, by thy fire divine*
> *Melt into tears this thankless heart of mine.*
> *Teach me to love what once I seemed to hate,*
> *And live for God before it be too late.*

God's love transcended all that my thankless heart had done to him. The truth of that love broke me and brought me to the Cross, where I sobbed my way home! The love of my parents and sister was one thing; the love of God was quite another. I realized that no man could ever love me enough, no child could ever love me enough, and no parent could ever care for me enough—only Jesus. He loved me so that I might love.

It is possible to live our entire lives as if Christ had not died for us. Plenty of people do just that. But many times this happens because they have not heard a clear presentation of the gospel. Loving God includes making sure people around us hear the good news that Jesus loves them, died for them, and wants to forgive their sins and come into their lives.

THE BATTLE TO LOVE

God knows how to love. He is very practiced at the art because he has been doing it forever! By giving us Christ by his Spirit, he has given us the power to love as he does.

Our problem is that we try to love each other using our own phileo love, which is friendship love, or eros love, which is sensual love. We need to put our human loves into the hands of God and submit them to him. We must ask him to rule and fuel them, to govern them, and to command them to obey. This way we are not relying on our own energy to sustain the kind of love only God can sustain.

In this book I want to talk about some of the loves of our lives. Love for a spouse, for children, for parents, and for friends. Love for the church, for the lost, and for the found. Love for rich little poor people and for poor little rich people. Love for mission and love for work. And of course, love for grandchildren!

As I take a backward look at my life and a forward look at my future, lacing all this together is my love for God and his precious Son, the Lord Jesus Christ. My poor, human love has been fanned into flame by his grace and his Spirit. He is the secret and source of all my other loves. Loving God comes first. Loving him is our primary calling. To love him in the happy times and the sad times, the rich times and the poor times, the young and the old times is the key to everything of worth in life.

And what of the battle to love? What about the selfish core of my heart that loves only me, supremely and arrogantly? Will I write of that? How can I not? For this is the battle of all battles; it is where we experience our greatest victories and our worst defeats. The problem is that we were born with a spy in the camp, an enemy within. We were born with a bias in our souls—a bias to self-centeredness, self-aggrandizement, self-absorption, self-indulgence, and self-destruction. This center core must be subdued by love— the love of God. Until I figure out how to let God get the victory in this battle over self, till love dominates my thinking, my actions, and my very soul, I will find no release.

The Bias to Sin

It's a bit like the game of bowls—not the bowling game you have in America but the staid and proper game that is played in England. This game consists of rolling a large black "bowl" (ball) toward a small white "jack" (a smaller white ball) on a superbly manicured piece of English grass called a "green." The idea is to get the big bowl as close as possible to the jack without touching it. This might sound really easy until you consider the fact that the bowl has a heavy weight (called a "bias") placed inside it. This bias constantly pulls it off center.

This is a good illustration of sin. Because we are born with this "bias" inside our souls, it doesn't matter how straight we are aimed at a target, or who aims us, sin pulls us off center! Our parents may do their best to keep us on course. Our Sunday school teachers or youth leaders may roll us as accurately as possible toward the goal, but that wretched, corrupted core is sometimes too strong for us. Time after time, we veer to the left or to the right.

I can testify to this. My parents aimed my sister and me in the right direction. They sent us to the best schools, were the best role models, taught us moral values, and let it be known they expected the best of us. Yet the bias of sin pulled me constantly off course.

When someone said right, I said wrong. When I was being taught the right way to live, I immediately tried to figure out a way to get around the system. No one explained that I was a weighted "bowl" with a sin bias working against me! So I rationalized what my conscience told me was wrong and called it "growing up" instead! I chloroformed my conscience and sinned as often as I saw fit, hoping my parents would not find out!

My sister did a better job of staying on course than I did. She warned me that it would kill Dad if I got pregnant or was caught cheating at exams. That salutary warning caused me brief concern, but the world opening up to me was too exciting to let these minor details trouble me for too long. Soon I was happily careening off course again. I have nothing and no one to blame but myself for the deceit and sin that I began to enjoy.

The Autumn of Discontent

Sin is pleasurable; otherwise we wouldn't be so tempted! The Bible tells us that Moses "chose to be mistreated along with the people of God rather than to enjoy the pleasures of sin for a short time" (Hebrews 11:25, NIV). However, the devil doesn't tell us that sin's pleasures last only for a short season! After a summer of fun comes the autumn of discontent followed by the winter of despair.

This wretched bias to self-gratification needs a counterbias. But we can't do it on our own. We need the presence of Jesus within us. When he lives his life in us, sin will not have dominion over us. A change will take place that gives us the power to love God and love others. What joy! What release and relief!

So where do you see yourself? Struggling with the bias you were born with? Practicing deceit? Enjoying the pleasures of sin? Rationalizing it all and calling it "being mature"? Would you like to be free of such self-obsession? Christ can set you free! Just ask him. Borrow my words if it helps.

> Lord Jesus, I am tired of it all. Forgive me for my self-worship. Come into my life and counter my horrible bias of sin. Set me free! Free to live for you and free to love for you. Scatter your love abroad in my heart by your Spirit as you promised to do. Thank you, Lord, for hearing and answering this prayer. Amen.

You see, we cannot live the Christian life. There is only one person who ever did, and that person is Jesus Christ. We can try to imitate his life—the way he worked, the way he thought, the way he cared for people, and above all, the way he loved people—but we will severely fail.

There is a story told of a small boy who was given a hen as a pet. The small hen produced small eggs. One day the boy was at the zoo, where a large ostrich had just produced an egg. It was a large egg, but then what would you expect from a large bird! The little boy took a picture and had it developed. He took his photo down to the little hen, propped it up in front of her, and said, "Look at this and try harder!"

It is useless to prop up a picture of Jesus in front of people and say, "Look at this and try harder!" For this they need Jesus. But if you have just repeated the prayer I suggested, then for this you have Jesus! Once he is resident, he needs to be president. He must be King of kings and Lord of lords! He must master you so you can master yourself. He must be obeyed gladly and willingly, whatever he asks you to do. As he fills every part of your life, you will find yourself capable of doing things you have given up hope of ever doing. Things like loving him back, and loving your friends and enemies alike.

Whom do you need to love? God himself? Do you need more love than you can find for a child, a relative, a friend, or an enemy? I pray that by the time we have shared this book together, you will know the reality of God's love for every person you know!

MAKING IT MINE

These questions can be used for personal quiet time or adapted for group discussions. A notebook, a Bible, and a pencil would be useful.

Thinking It Over

1. Review the chapter. Which part of it alerted you to a problem in your life? Pause and pray about it.
2. Discuss or write a sentence about agape, phileo, and eros love. Define them in your own words.
3. Think about the illustration of the small hen and the ostrich egg. Why was it silly of the boy to expect the hen to "try harder"? How can you apply this illustration?
4. Do you know the Lord? Did you say the prayer to accept him into your life? Write a thank-you note to God about that.
5. Read I John 4:7-11. Do you believe it? Memorize it.
6. Make a list of ten people in your life you need to love. Thank God in advance for what he will do for them through you.

Praying It In

1. Be still and quiet until your focus changes from you to him. Don't move until you don't want to! Savor it.
2. Do you think you are more often focused on yourself than on anyone or anything else? Do *you* dominate your thinking? Would you like to change? Pray about that!
3. Think about the most difficult person to love in your life. Have you given up trying to love him or her? Why? Will you try again? Pray about that.

Prayer

Lord, I need you every hour. I need you to love you! Fill my heart with gratitude for your love. Keep me honest. Change my focus from myself to others. Give me release from being a prisoner of my own world, and help me see the people that you need me to love. Then give me the ability to love them.

Show me how to live in this world of love. Make me restless till I know what it is to love you with all of my heart, soul, mind, and strength. I want to feel the wind of your Spirit in my sails, your Word in my mind, and your love in my heart every moment of every daily day. I cannot do this without Jesus. But for this I have Jesus! How can I ever say thanks? I love you the best that I know how, but I want to love the best that you know I can! Work this work in me, Lord. I submit my will to yours. Amen.

Living It Out

1. Think of one person who needs to hear something you have read in this chapter.
2. Make an action plan. When will you share this with that person? How will you share it?
3. Do it!

CHAPTER TWO

LOVING WHEN THE LOVE RUNS OUT

My command is this:
Love each other as I have loved you.
JOHN 15:12 (NIV)

MARRIAGE CAN BE HARD WORK. AS THE YOUNG GIRLS ON A Christian campus seemed to be saying, "Mom and dad couldn't make it, so what makes us think we have what it takes to make a marriage work?"

What do we do when the love runs out? Do we run out too? It's easy these days to do just that. The stigma associated with divorce is almost gone. Tolerance is the prevailing virtue—or even the "eleventh commandment." Yet when we can no longer tolerate our spouse, when the love runs out, we can just walk away!

OPPOSITES ATTRACT

There are obviously as many reasons for the breakdown of marriages today as there are people in those marriages. But one of the most often quoted reasons for divorce is "irreconcilable differences."

"We were too different," explained a young woman who had come to talk to me about her failing marriage. "But we didn't know we were until he got me home and the door shut behind us!"

"How long were you engaged?" I asked her.

"Three months, but we had known each other for two years," she replied somewhat defensively.

"But didn't you work in different parts of the state and only see each other on weekends?" I asked.

"Yes, but we had all our weekends and holidays together."

Holidays and weekends. Not a lot of time to really get to know a person, to see the "whole package," so to speak; not a lot of time to see potential problems and work them out ahead of marriage.

In the old days, not necessarily the *good* old days, a courtship and engagement would be the time to get some of the bugs out of the relationship before tying the knot. For example, it can be a good idea not to walk into marriage with money problems and debt. Sometimes, however, that's just too long to wait, as this little poem illustrates:

> *The bride bent with age leaned over her cane,*
> *Her steps so uncertain need guiding,*
> *While down the church aisle*
> *With a wan toothless smile*
> *The groom in a wheelchair came gliding.*
>
> *And who is this elderly couple thus wed?*
> *You'll find when you've quickly explored it*
> *That this is that rare most unusual pair*
> *Who waited till they could afford it!*
> —Anonymous

I shared this piece of prize poetry with my young friend, and she gave a little grimace and shook her head. "Well, we couldn't afford it; in fact, both of us had school loans to pay off, but we went ahead anyway," she said.

"How long had you spent just being friends?" I asked next. She looked at me, not understanding the question. "Friendship is the place to explore the people we are, learn to celebrate our differences, and come to terms with them," I explained. "A good marriage is made up of two good friends, two good forgivers, and two good Jesus lovers and glory givers! Did anyone tell you that you spend very little time in the bedroom when you are married?" I inquired.

She looked at me wide eyed.

"I suspect," I continued, "you had a hot romance and struggled to keep control of the sexual side of things. In fact, you may have

22

put all your energy into trying to do that and spent precious little time developing friendship. Friendship is the place for discovery and acceptance. It's the place you laugh together, cry together, and just plain have fun together. It's the place you learn not to take yourself too seriously—which is so very important in marriage. In fact, if you don't learn to laugh at yourself and with your friend, it's going to be tough making a marriage work. Do you know how to enjoy a good laugh together?"

"No," she said sadly, "and I think it's too late. There's sure nothing to laugh about now. You are right. We met, fell in love, struggled with our sexual relationship, and decided the sooner we got married the better. The engagement period was taken up with wedding arrangements, and now we have only been married a year and we don't love each other anymore. We have found out that we have nothing in common; in fact, we are total opposites! Why didn't we see that before?"

"You didn't give yourselves a chance to, that's why," I replied. "Opposites attract! Then they get married. Wait awhile, and opposites will begin to drive each other crazy! Why? It's because we are all inherently selfish. It is that bias to self-centeredness that comes with us to the altar, accompanies us on the honeymoon, and moves into "happily ever after" without our taking note that it is present.

"Self is interested only in its own things, not in the things of others. Self wants to do only the things *it* is interested in doing, see the videos *it* wants to watch, vacation where *it* has always vacationed, spend its free time doing what *it* wants to do. If it meets or, worse, marries a person who doesn't think as it thinks, make decisions as it makes decisions, or listen to its conversation all the time, it pouts, throws a tantrum, or runs out of the room!"

Now I had the young woman's full attention!

"That's what self does, but to be honest, that often describes me," I said. "If I can't have my own way, I throw a fit!" We laughed. That was better. I figured it had been awhile since she had cracked a smile. We talked, prayed, and parted company. She promised to come back and talk some more. I hoped we could see a marriage saved. Only God knew the future.

APPRECIATING OUR DIFFERENCES

Marriage reveals that we are very different people. It takes God to help us handle—even appreciate—our differences. It's not easy to have a very different person living in our lives, up close and personal!

Stuart and I are very different. You can tell just how different we are by looking at the titles of our books! Stuart is very positive by nature. He is an optimist, so he gives his books grand titles such as, *What Works When Life Doesn't* or *Eight Ways to Get a Life.*

My work, on the other hand, reflects my natural tendency toward introspection, a sober spirit, and morbid thought patterns! So I have written books on Job, Jeremiah, and Lamentations, as well as a children's book about suffering called *Harrow Sparrow*, which is a harrowing tale indeed! We are different in temperament and work habits; in fact, we are direct opposites. He always assumes the best; I always anticipate the worst.

Not long ago, Stuart and I were in a hotel in Chicago. In the middle of the night, the fire alarm went off. I leapt out of bed, threw myself into my best suit, grabbed my purse, computer, Bible, and notes and took off down the fire escape. Stuart followed leisurely in his shorts and T-shirt and didn't even bring his wallet! He was sure it was a false alarm. Actually, it *was* a false alarm, but the incident highlighted our differences. As he joined me outside, he looked at me knowingly, and we both laughed.

We have not, however, allowed our differences to irritate but rather have learned with God's help to celebrate and delight in them. For this we have needed Jesus, but for this we have had Jesus! Love always accepts the differences in others as a challenge and delight. Self always imagines everyone should be like it. Love thinks differently and allows others to do the same.

Paul talks about "growing up" out of our inherent selfishness into selflessness. "Love does not demand its own way," he writes in I Corinthians 13:5. He tells the Corinthians that they cannot make love work unless they grow up and mature. Mature love is not selfish! Look again at the verse we talked about in the previous chapter. The apostle said, "When I was a child, I spoke and thought and reasoned as a child does. But when I grew up, I put away childish things" (I Corinthians 13:11). To be selfish is to act like a child; in order to love, you need to grow up and put away childish selfishness!

Unfortunately, people who have never grown up are getting married. There are so many kids getting married. That is the problem. They might be eighteen-year-old kids, thirty-year-old kids, or fifty-year-old kids, but they behave like children. Marriage is not intended for children because the prevailing attitude of children is selfishness. I know—I ran a preschool for three hundred children for ten years. I became very familiar with their behavior. I can't tell you how many times in thirty years of ministry I have sat in marriage counseling sessions and felt as though I were back in my classroom trying to sort out squabbles that belonged in preschool! If we don't grow up and put childish ways behind us, our relationships are in for a rough ride.

One day we were visiting a family we hadn't seen for a long time. The older children were bringing us up to speed on their lives and telling us their plans for the future, while the four-year-old waited impatiently for a pause in the conversation. His father noticed his dilemma and said to him, "Duncan, tell Pastor Briscoe what you want to be when you grow up." Duncan thought for a moment and then said, "Bigger!"

That was a noble aspiration. Oh, that all of us were like Duncan, that all of us would want to be bigger people and grow up into mature human beings. We all need to grow up in the art of loving. If we don't, we will live lives that are inherently selfish. Do you want to be "bigger" in the matter of loving? I do.

LOVE BEGINS WITH FRIENDSHIP
Friendship is a great place to grow up into love! Selfishness can safely be worked out in the arena of friendship. Perhaps you can

learn to watch sports with your husband or go shopping with your wife. Work on learning something new together.

Stuart and I chose a hobby neither of us knew anything about—bird watching. We learned it together. It was fun and relaxing and totally different from anything else we had done. We were on level ground; one of us was not an "expert" helping the other.

You may not have a marriage that is falling apart, but if you are honest, you might not be able to say that you and your spouse are good friends. This may be because you don't play together, find a common goal, laugh together, or just plain have fun. You may need to give yourselves time to rediscover friendship.

When our daughter Judy wanted to get engaged, she called home to talk to us. She and Greg were at Wheaton College and had been dating for three years. They had put their eros love on the back burner for obvious reasons and had been working hard at their friendship. Now they were facing graduation, and it was time to talk about marriage.

"Daddy," she began, "can I marry my best friend?" I would venture to say many parents would have welcomed that question! We were grateful for Judy and Greg's maturity and integrity.

"There has to be attraction, too," Stuart ventured, "but if there is, then you have one of the most important things in place for a good marriage—your abiding friendship with Greg." Nineteen years of marriage and three children later, their friendship is deeper and more multifaceted than ever. It has been an anchor for the soul of a marriage that has real substance and satisfaction.

GOD CAN TRANSFORM OUR LOVES
A good marriage needs to be built on more than just friendship and attraction, however. Greg and Judy have Jesus, and so they have learned to show agape love as well. Friendship love—phileo—alone cannot sustain a marriage; hot romance—eros—will eventually cool. Every marriage that is as God intended it to be needs to submit its human loves to God so that he can transform them. Let phileo submit to agape; let eros submit as well. If they don't, then when

friendship wanes or sexual satisfaction fades, marriage walks out the door. Agape must rule and fuel a marriage. Agape can hold a marriage together when the friends are in a fight or when the lovers feel ice cold. Agape alone can stir the dying embers back into flame.

In his book *Love Within Limits* (Grand Rapids: Eerdmans, 1978), Lewis Smedes writes:

> Agape is the power for sticking with a marriage when the passion has burned down to dreary toleration. It is the power to wait and see if desire might be ignited, and eros re-created later. Agape is the energy to do the work of eros, even when the feelings of eros are gone. . . .
>
> Agape forgives the guilty spouse, affirms the unlovely spouse, bears with bad taste, insensitive neglect, stupid decisions, and cruel aggressiveness. . . . Agape cannot create a marriage, but it can carry a marriage when eros is cold. (102)

If we are divorced from the source of love, God himself, we do not have what it takes to sustain self-sacrificial love. Of course, we all know couples who do not believe in God and yet have stayed happily married all their lives. We may know the love of parents or siblings who don't believe. But even in their finest moments, phileo (human love) and eros (sexual love) are tinged with selfishness. They need the help of agape to reach outside themselves to others and give themselves away.

The fact is, when the wind blows and trouble comes, we need a source of love well beyond our human capacity. If we submit our human loves to God, he will transform them because he transcends them. If we let him govern our marriages, we will find a reservoir of love we didn't believe could exist. If he rules our loves, he will fuel our loves.

MARRIAGE IS GOD'S IDEA

The thing about loving your spouse is that you can know that God is on your side. That is because marriage is his idea. All God's ideas are good and gracious. Marriage matters to God. And if God matters to you, then the things that matter to him should matter to you.

Jesus sanctified marriage not only by talking about it but also by going to a wedding. It happened right at the beginning of his ministry (see John 2:1-11). In fact, it was the occasion of his first miracle. It was a happy miracle at a happy occasion, and it gives us a good analogy.

Jesus and the disciples were invited to a wedding in Cana of Galilee. Jesus' mother was there as well. The ritual at an Eastern wedding in Jesus' time was very different from our way of doing things today. The master of ceremonies (John 2:9) was responsible for all the proceedings. He ran the show. Not only would he lose face, but the bridegroom's family would be subject to jesting for years to come if anything went wrong with the food or the wine at such an event. At this particular wedding, that's what happened. The wine ran out!

Jesus was a guest. He was not the master of ceremonies. But when Mary learned that the wine had run out, she told the servants to "do whatever [Jesus] tells you" (John 2:5). Basically she was telling the servants that if they put the whole situation in Jesus' hands and obeyed him, he would take care of it.

They took her advice, and Jesus took charge. He told the servants to fill the large empty waterpots with water. Then he instructed them to dip some out and take it to the master of ceremonies. Jesus had turned the water into wine! The master of ceremonies was astounded (and surely relieved). "Usually a host serves the best wine first. . . . But you have kept the best until now!" he said to the bridegroom (John 2:10). Neither of them had any idea what was happening back in the kitchen!

Here is the analogy. Many people invite Jesus to their wedding, but only as a guest. They want God to bless but not to boss! They want a church wedding in a church building. They want God to attend and even want to borrow his house for the ceremony. In England many people still want church weddings even though they never darken the doors of a church for the rest of their days apart from baptisms and funerals! This is a long way from wanting Christ to be the Master of their marriage.

When Stuart and I served a local church, which we did for thirty years, my husband often got calls at the parsonage from people looking in the yellow pages for a church for the wedding ceremony and a pastor to officiate. We used to call these "yellow-pages weddings"! "Do you do weddings?" they would ask.

"No," he would reply, "but I institute Christian marriages!" This often proved to be a great opportunity to explain both what a real Christian was and what the biblical idea of marriage is all about. It was also a great opportunity to minister to young couples and lead them to Christ. This way the couple had a chance to build their marriage on the best possible foundation.

So is Jesus the Master of your marriage? Is he in charge? Are you in a difficult marriage today? Has the "wine run out"? Turn it over to Jesus. He'll know what to do, just as Mary said.

GOD IS REALLY GOOD AT MIRACLES

Many more calls come to the parsonage about marriages that are in progress but are not "progressing" very well. I remember one such call that I received.

"I want a divorce!" the lady announced loudly and angrily.

"My husband doesn't do divorces," I replied. "He is a pastor. He institutes Christian marriages. He tries to help people who are in trouble in their relationships as well."

"It's too late," she replied brusquely. "We are incompatible."

"Don't you know that incompatibility is the reason for marriage, not divorce?" I asked. "Let's talk." I told her that Jesus can turn water into wine! "Sometimes," I said, "when the 'wine' runs out of a relationship and everything becomes flat and ordinary, Jesus can bring the taste and sparkle back, whatever the problem is."

"Have you seen this happen?" she asked me seriously.

"Yes," I told her. "Some marriages are down to a miracle, but God is really good at miracles. He invented them!"

Like the young woman who came to see me about her marriage crisis, or the desperate lady on the phone, many people have lost hope of anything happening to save their marriages. Many couples have set off in grand style to live happily ever after, only to see their highest hopes and dreams crumble. They have put all their human energy into making it work, but phileo love by itself cannot sustain a relationship. It can sustain it on a certain level, but when trouble comes, something more than mere human love is needed. And when the marriage is in trouble, eros love is completely set aside.

But God is a God of miracles. I have watched some couples turn to God in desperation and ask him to save their marriages. As they have invited him to take his rightful place as Master of their lives and loves, he has done his healing work.

Sometimes the master of ceremonies of a wedding in Jesus' day would sit between the bride and the groom to preside over the event and make sure nothing went amiss. When Stuart and I married, we used that picture when we bought our wedding rings. We purchased three stones. The middle one represents Jesus, and the ones on each side represent Stuart and me. Every day I am reminded that if we keep Jesus at the center of our marriage, it will work!

How does this play out? Well, if you lose your temper with your spouse, you will remember that the Bible says, "Don't let the sun go down while you are still angry" (Ephesians 4:26). In other words, don't go to sleep without putting things right. Say your "sorrys" before you put out the light. Keep short accounts with your spouse, and don't let a whole lot of unresolved things pile up, creating unseen barriers between you.

Perhaps you are upset with your spouse. You begin internally justifying yourself and mentally putting your partner down. You judge his or her actions, giving a day or two of stony silence for punishment. But the Bible says, "Do not judge, and you will not be judged. Do not condemn, and you will not be condemned. Forgive, and you will be forgiven" (Luke 6:37, NIV). Christ is sitting in the judgment seat and Christ alone. So let him be the judge of your spouse's behavior. By all means, express your feelings and what you think about the matter, but in love! Then always be willing to forgive as God has forgiven you. Love is gentle and kind, forgiving and forbearing. It doesn't keep a running record of the other person's wrongs but is quick to see the best in people. Letting agape govern your reactions to your spouse will transform your marriage.

MARRIAGE IS FOR KEEPS

To make a marriage work, we need to keep God's rules for marriage. What are these rules? One of the most important rules is that marriage is for keeps. Any question of breaking the bond is to be considered unthinkable and nonnegotiable!

Not long ago a Christian couple came to see my husband and me and talked about the serious problems they were experiencing. This husband and wife were well known in evangelical circles. They were at the point where they were talking about the possibility of divorce. I remember the shock this was to me. From the outside, no one would have guessed that they were in trouble. It made me wonder how many more Christian couples were struggling to such a degree.

My husband began to work toward a commitment to the "no option out" rule. If we could get both of them to commit to this, then some other skilled counselor could help them from there. It was early in the morning before my husband used an illustration that helped to take them over that line of submitting to the governing principles of the Lord.

"Think of two people trapped in a burning building," he said. "Both have a key to the fire escape. The obvious and practical thing to do is to use their 'out' and escape the heat. Given the situation, no one would blame them for escaping from a seemingly intolerable situation.

"Your marriage is at this point," Stuart continued. "It is being destroyed, and you both feel trapped in this burning building. But you both have the key to the fire escape in your hands. Knowing what you have told us tonight, many people would not blame you if you used it. But if both of you will come to the point of throwing away the keys to the fire escape, then you will have no alternative but to fight the flames together!"

There was silence in the room. It was show time. I sat there as still as could be, praying like mad, as first the woman and then the man said through their tears, "God helping me, I will throw away my option to escape from this marriage. I will fight the flames."

That marriage was saved. God worked in that hotel room and became Master of a situation where the "wine" had run out of the relationship years ago. They took action and recommitted themselves to each other for many reasons, not least because they loved and served the Lord and his honor was at stake. The motivating force in their decision was sheer obedience to the Christ they both loved and served. Their ministry, which could have been destroyed, blossomed and flourished, as did their relationship.

God can turn what has become stale water into sparkling wine. If you are reading this book and are in the burning building of your marriage, will you throw that key away? It takes two, I know. But you can start to do your part, in faith praying that God will work a "Cana" miracle for you. When we're willing to live by the rule that marriage is for keeps, God has a chance to make our marriages work!

> Love fights the flames.
> Love laughs at impossibilities, ignores the heat, rolls up its spiritual sleeves, and gets to work.
> Love throws the key to the fire escape out the window and looks for a bucket of water. Love finds it, for it has been there all the time waiting to be used. God has put it close at hand.
> Love fights on, determined to see God get the glory. God gets the glory when his rules are obeyed. When love is triumphant, people living in all the other burning buildings on the street, and whose own houses are on fire, see the flames extinguished and gain hope.
> Love fights the flames.

Don't wait for the other person to start fighting the flames. You throw your key out the window first. Start to put out the flames around your own feet. Maybe you have actually been fueling the flames. Perhaps habits need changing. Ask God to show you where to start fighting the fire.

Once the immediate danger has passed, there will be a lot of rubble to remove because a lot of damage has been done. Clearing up the mess and rebuilding will take time and energy. But love has all the time in the world and all the divine energy necessary to accomplish the goal. Love is the greatest firefighter!

Love is very patient. That's how love is, and that's what love does—patiently loves a relationship back to robust health. Love never fails to go on loving. It can outlast anything.

God gave us the rule of love. His rules matter to him, and if they matter to him, they should matter to us. If we obey them, our marriages will work. If we break his rules, nothing will work.

Marriage is precious to him, and because he is precious to me, my marriage is precious to me. It helps me to know that when I break something precious to him, I hurt him. That stops my destructive habits in a hurry. If you are busy breaking your marriage vows, pause to hear him say, "By breaking your marriage vows, you are breaking my heart!"

The story is told of a small child who was left alone in the care of his grandfather. Taking a few moments out for himself, the grandfather went to make a cup of tea. There was a loud crash, and a special vase lay shattered on the ground. The child took one look at the grandfather's face and set off running, but there was nowhere to go. The little one paused, turned around, and flew into his grandfather's arms sobbing, "I'm sowwy, I'm sowwy, Papa!" The grandfather swept up the child and held him against his chest, soothing him and murmuring, "It's all right. I love you! I forgive you. Now let's sweep up the mess." As the grandfather stood there calming the little boy, he seemed to hear his heavenly Father say, "Why can't you do that? Why can't you turn around and fly into my waiting arms?"

Well, why can't you? If you have broken something that is precious to God, like your marriage vows, don't run. Turn around and fly into your heavenly Father's arms. He's waiting—and you will wish you had come sooner! He will forgive you, and together you can start to sweep up the mess.

Sometimes the precious thing that has been broken can be mended, and sometimes it cannot. But you can start with you. Do your part and leave the rest to him. God is a mender of things that are broken. "He heals the brokenhearted, binding up their wounds"

(Psalm 147:3). When people learn to turn to the Heart Mender, miracles can happen.

THE BEST IS YET TO COME

Many marriages peak. They grow to a certain point and then settle for the mediocre and just coast. There is mutual tolerance, but what kind of life is that? Who wants to live in a marriage that is lukewarm at best? Jesus doesn't want lukewarm love; in fact, he tells the church in Laodicea that their lukewarm love for him makes him sick (Revelation 3:16). If lukewarm love for God upsets him, it follows that lukewarm love between his people upsets him, too.

Have you gone from hot to lukewarm—or even to freezing? It can get better. Don't despair. Every Christian marriage needs to have the positive hope that, however long you've been married, the best is yet to come!

The master of ceremonies at the wedding feast in Cana told the bridegroom, "You have kept the best until now" (John 2:10). I have asked the Master of our marriage feast to let Stuart and me say that too! We have been married forty-five years. Stuart is in his seventies, and I am in my sixties. But I believe the best is yet to come! What fun! We can't wait to discover new heights and depths to the dimensions of the love of God we have already experienced and the sweet overflow of that love into our marriage.

Don't settle for anything else! The difference with Christian couples is that they have the One who invented marriage on their side. He doesn't want you to settle for the mundane. He wants to turn the water into wine. I say to those of you in marriages that are safe yet dull—it doesn't need to be like this! The best is yet to come. Here are some helpful steps to renewal in a marriage:

Tell Jesus about It
Go to him, like Mary, his mother, did and tell him the problem. Be honest. Say, "Lord, the wine has run out." That's all you need to say. He knows it anyway, but he wants you to address the issue.

Listen to His Instructions

How will you hear them? Will you hear a voice in your head? I don't know. God might address you through an idea that comes into your mind, but a more sure way is through his Word. So be reading the Bible every day, and be aware that you may read something that directly speaks to the issue. You may read a principle that needs to be put into practice. God works through people, too. It may be you want to share some of these things with a godly person, your pastor, or a gifted marriage counselor.

Be Obedient

Once you figure out the first thing to do, do it! Mary said, "Do whatever he tells you." It might be that you need to work on your communication or your sex life. If one partner has had sexual issues in the past and has never dealt with them, these can affect his or her attitudes toward intimacy. These wounds from the past need healing. Work together to take the necessary steps.

Pray about Everything

Praying together is hard for many couples, even for those in full-time ministry. If praying together is difficult, then pray individually—but pray!

Remember Agape

Agape love always seeks the good of the other first, so ask God to show you one thing that only you can do for your spouse.

THE AUTUMN OF MARRIAGE

I was browsing through one of the books I wrote at least twenty-five years ago. The book was about growing older—not growing old, but growing older. There is a difference! Under a lovely picture of a sunset I had written, "God paints his choicest colors in his latest sunsets." I thought about that. He wants to use his renewing paintbrush not only in your life but also in your marriage. He wants you to discover love in its entire grand dimensions, the longer you live and the longer you are married.

God has certainly painted his choicest colors in our marriage in its latest days. The reason? We have tried—imperfectly, but we've tried anyway—to follow his rules of love. We have sought to submit our human love for each other to the rule of agape. We have tried to be obedient to God's rules of marriage. We have found all the power and all the love we need for each other in him!

Not long ago Stuart and I were busy speaking at different venues in the course of ministry. He was in the South trying to get to California, and I was in Milwaukee trying to get to Boston. We both ended up with cancelled planes and a five-hour layover in Chicago's O'Hare airport. Neither of us knew this, of course. We sat down and got our work out to pass the time. It was one of those days that has been a part of our lives for over forty years of ministry. We were apart from each other once again.

After I had worked on a manuscript for a good thirty minutes, I started to think about Stuart. *I wish he were here with me,* I thought. I looked at my watch and reasoned that he would have arrived in California for his next assignment. So I got out my new cell phone and thought I would try to reach him. As the phone rang, he got up opposite me! I screamed out, "Oh, it's you!" We laughed and laughed, and he came and gave me a big kiss!

This really set people looking as we had both sat there for at least half an hour! Seeing these apparent strangers kissing and laughing got their attention. How good of God to work out this wonderful serendipity for us. In an airport the size of O'Hare, we could have never crossed paths. Instead, we walked the long concourses as if they were a green meadow and had lunch at our favorite bagel stand. We spent a wonderful afternoon together until our planes left. I can't tell you how my heart leapt just to see "my man" there so unexpectedly! Truly, when Christ governs your life and your marriage, it gets better and better as time goes on.

Where are you in your life's cycle? Have you just gotten married? Has God just begun to paint your marriage on his canvas? Then you are living in springtime. Have you been on the way a little while? Have you been blessed with a couple of kids, a good job, and a nice place to live? Then summer is upon you. Or maybe you are in what seems like autumn—the leaves have begun to turn brown, and an ominous wind has arisen. Or perhaps you are living in full-blown winter, and everything is frozen, miserable, and cold.

To those of you living in springtime, be alert! Know that you have an enemy of your souls and an enemy of your marriage. It is not for nothing that Jesus called Satan "a murderer from the beginning" (John 8:44). Satan wants to kill your marriage. Make sure that you build into your relationship a spiritual dimension and make it the most important aspect of your lives. God will give you weapons to defend yourselves against all the forces that would tear your marriage apart. Spend time thinking about the wedding at Cana. Is Jesus Master of your marriage? If not, make him so. You do that by inviting him to be in control and, as best you know how, asking him to rule your marriage.

If you are in summer mode, revisit the things that really matter but may be neglected. Reexamine your values and your lifestyle, and see if they are compatible with your profession of Christianity. Maybe plan to have a spiritual or marital checkup. Make any midcourse corrections you need to make. Read a good marriage enrichment book together. Go to a couples conference, or see a counselor to help you discern any warning signs.

I know a couple who were given some money for a Christmas gift. Their marriage was in good shape. They were in Christian ministry and loved it and each other. They had been married about fifteen years. They decided to spend the money on a marriage counselor. They felt a little foolish walking into his office hand in hand, but they went ahead and hoped the man would not feel that they were wasting his time. The counselor was delighted! It was a relief and an encouragement to him that they were determined not to allow their marriage to descend into mediocrity. They were young and healthy and wanted to make a good marriage as good as it could be. The couple said those sessions were well worth the money, and both received invaluable help in marriage enrichment. They finished the course and left the office saying and believing, "The best is yet to come!"

If you are in the autumn of a relationship, take action! Don't wait. Turn around and run into the waiting arms of God. Do your part in saying your "sorrys" to him, and then say them to your spouse. Own your part and remember that you are responsible only for your response and reactions, not anyone else's. Agape doesn't wait for the other person to make the first move. Agape runs to make amends. Don't give up, for the best is yet to come.

God would save us from winter—from the frost and cold and misery. He has better things in mind. All of us know about the miracle of the springtime. We expect it, don't we? Then expect the miracle of resurrection in the winter of your marriage. God is a God of miracles.

MAKING IT MINE

These questions can be used for personal quiet time or adapted for group discussions. A notebook, a Bible, and a pencil would be useful.

Thinking It Over

1. Where are you in your marriage relationship—in the springtime, summer, autumn, or winter? Write a short letter to God about where you find yourself and one request where you need his help.
2. Read the account of the wedding at Cana in John 2. Discuss or make a list of the things that apply to your married life from this true story.
3. Read Genesis 2:24-25. What does God say about marriage? Read Mark 10:6-9. What does Jesus add about marriage to the Genesis comments? Which part of these verses struck you and why?
4. What makes us settle for less than the best in our marriages?
5. Do you have a premarital course in your church? If not, what should it contain? Why not start one? Prevention is better than a cure.

Praying It In

1. Make a list of people whose marriages need prayer. Spend five minutes praying for them.
2. Spend time being still in Agape's presence. Let him make you aware of his love! Praise him for the boundless possibilities that lie ahead.

Prayer

Thank you for the privilege of marriage, Lord. Sometimes I am tempted to think of it as punishment rather than a privilege, but your Word tells me marriage is your idea. Give me back the grand sense of privilege I once knew.

I think I need to get a biblical perspective on my relationship, Lord, so give me some help on this. Show me where to look in Scripture for some practical principles. Help me to play by the rules—your rules—and to be obedient to the precepts I find. Teach me what agape love is all about. Teach me to submit my human love to you to keep it fresh and pure.

I pray for my partner, Lord. We need your help. Give us the desire to seek after your heart, Lord. Don't let us settle for a lukewarm love. Make us determined to do the work that needs to be done. Turn this water into wine!

Make our marriage better than anything we have had before. No more cheap wine, Lord. No more cheap wine! Hear my prayer, for I want to honor you in my marriage so you get the glory due to your name. I pray this for Christ's sake. Amen.

Living It Out

1. What one action are you going to take away with you from this chapter? When will you start? How will you do it?
2. If you need to talk to a person about any of this, who will that person be? When will you make an appointment?

CHAPTER THREE
LOVING THE CHURCH
(EVEN WHEN IT'S DIFFICULT)

Christ loved the church and gave himself up for her.
EPHESIANS 5:25 (NIV)

PAUL'S EXQUISITE CHAPTER ON LOVE, 1 CORINTHIANS 13, comes in the middle of a letter to the church in the city of Corinth. This church had begun with a group of people who heard the gospel through his preaching, believed it, and received the Holy Spirit into their lives. They began to meet together and to love and care for each other as they followed Jesus. Paul helped them to find leaders from among themselves whom God had gifted by his Spirit to teach and guide them.

The problem with the church at Corinth was that it didn't mature very quickly. It was a church full of immature Christian "babies" bickering with each other. So Paul, hearing about their problems, sat down to write a letter to straighten them out.

Having lots of little children in one place can be a wild experience! There was a time in our family when our children got married and began to produce their own children at alarmingly regular intervals. At one point, three babies were born within twenty-four hours! Our daughter gave birth to Drew, and our son Dave and his wife had twins named Christy and David. These three children have stayed very close through the years. When they were two years of age, we renamed the three of them Search, Destroy, and Demolition! When they were two years old, it was cute. Obviously, we expected them to grow up and receive their proper names back!

When people are born again, they begin as spiritual "babies," and we make allowances for a certain amount of childish behavior. However, if they are still named Search, Destroy, and Demolition in the church family thirty years later, we have a big problem on our hands! Maybe you have a Search, Destroy, and Demolition in your church.

As the church was born at Pentecost, some believers grew up rapidly. As they showed agape love to each other, the people around them noticed how they loved one another. The people watching the Corinthian church, however, were noticing how the believers argued with one another! What do the people around your church say about you? Loving the church is a challenge. Loving the people in the church can be very difficult indeed.

A BAD CASE OF "FLOCK SHOCK"

A group of young people and I were talking to some kids as we wandered around a theme park. As we tried to tell them about Christ, they showed interest as long as we kept the conversation on him. They were all for Jesus Christ, but as soon as the subject of the church came up, their interest waned, and some became downright hostile.

"I'm all for Jesus, but you can keep the church," commented a kid who I discovered had never once been inside a church building! How could the church have had such bad press? I wondered. And how, as my husband often says, can you be all for Jesus Christ but not all for what he is for? As we talked with these youngsters far into the night, most of them had a horror story to tell about the church. They were suffering from a bad case of "flock shock."

Have you ever suffered from flock shock? The flock of God, the church, can heal and help, but it can also dismay and disappoint.

When I first became a Christian, I had never attended a church. My school taught Scripture and took us to church at Easter and Pentecost. However, the headmistress had let it be known that she didn't believe much in the church, so we students followed suit. Growing up in postwar Britain, no one in my age group and circle of friends actually made a habit of going to church regularly.

Then I came to Christ! Once I was born again, I was told I ought to join a church. That was okay by me, so I went home at the college semester break and told my folks I had become an active Christian and wanted to join a local church. I will always remember my parents' puzzled looks as they strove to understand what I was telling them.

"Which church will you join, Jill?" my mother asked me.

"I don't know," I replied. "What do you think?"

"Well," said my mother very seriously, "we're Presbyterians!"

I was delighted. "I didn't know," I said. "So where is our church?"

My mother looked it up in the paper, and the following Sunday I went off to "our church" for the first time. I was excited. However, by the end of the day I was in flock shock!

There were about ten people scattered around "our pews." The "flock" was certainly not flocking into this establishment. I couldn't hear anyone singing "our songs" because of our thunderous organ. It was winter, and the one heating pipe ran down the center of the building. The pillars holding up the ceiling of the church also ran down the middle of the structure, so we all took our places behind the pillars, put our frozen feet on the pipe, and tried to keep warm. I noticed the organist had gloves on! I didn't blame him. When the poor minister got up to preach, he couldn't see a soul because we were all out of sight. *How discouraging for him*, I thought.

After it was over (thank goodness), I went up to him and introduced myself. I told him I had had a conversion experience at Cambridge and wanted to join the church. He looked exceedingly doubtful and said I would need to start attending for a while before that would be possible.

As I complied and met the church people, I moved into a state of shock. Was this what Christ died for? There was no welcome for me and no encouragement to join this particular flock. I realize now that they didn't know what to do with me. I think it had been a long time since anyone "unchurched" had come near.

Fortunately, someone introduced me to a lively group of young believers at another church in the same denomination. My new Christian friends tempered my first bad impressions.

LOVING AND SERVING THE CHURCH

My husband says, "Church isn't somewhere you go; church is something you are." As I grew in God and was exposed to life as it ought to be in the body of believers, I began to understand the meaning of "Christ loved the church and gave himself up for her" (Ephesians 5:25, NIV). I understood that I was a member of his body, and he was the head. I saw in the Bible that the church is God's method of operation in this world, so I had better learn how to love and serve it!

But that is easier said than done. I kept bumping into people who had been hurt by the church. I found out at my own father's funeral that he had been upset in his youth by a split in a church that I didn't even know he had attended. He had sworn never to darken the door of a church again! He never did. "Flock shock" did him in.

Paul writes 1 Corinthians 13 to a church that could have given anybody flock shock. The Corinthian church was split by backbiting and controversy. The Christians there were "people followers," causing trouble in the ranks. They were immature and didn't know how to love each other. Yet the church was also filled with extremely gifted people, forgiven by God and indwelt by the Spirit. They needed tact and wisdom to know what to do with all the abilities they had been given, and that was the problem. All these gifted people were abusing their spiritual gifts and thus bringing discredit to God. They were using their gifts not for the Lord but rather for their own ends.

You see, spiritual gifts are tools God gives to his people to help him build his kingdom. Winston Churchill appealed to our allies in the Second World War, "Give us the tools, and we'll finish the job!" God has left us down here with a job to do. It is to tell a world without Christ about him.

I heard a fable about Jesus dying and returning to heaven. When he got there, the angels gathered around and asked him whom he had left in charge on earth. Jesus pointed out the eleven disciples. The angels were horrified. They had witnessed the disciples' behavior; they knew those men had forsaken Jesus and fled just when he had needed them the most. "Master," they asked, "what happens if they fail?"

"I have no other plans," Jesus replied.

It seems incredible that Jesus has left all of us failing people down here to do his work, but that is exactly what he has done. And what is more, he's promised to give us all that we need to finish the job. Once we are called to this task, the Spirit gives us the special tools we will need. He does not call those who already have it all together; rather, he equips those he has called with the tools they will need. Spiritual gifts are not toys, but that's how the Corinthians were acting—showing off, getting jealous, being prideful. That's because they were spiritual babies, and babies play with toys!

Hearing what was going on with the spiritually gifted Corinthians, Paul writes some pretty strong words to them in I Corinthians 14:20: "Don't be childish in your understanding of these things" (referring to the use and practice of spiritual gifts). In other words, "To be perfectly frank, I'm getting exasperated with your infantile thinking. How long before you grow up and use your head—your *adult* head?" (*The Message*).

The problem with this church was that the believers were using their gifts selfishly for their own ends. These people were used to living their lives out of their feelings. In the ancient world Corinth was called "the city of love." On the acropolis there was a temple where the people worshiped eros—the sexual, sensual side of love. So it is easy to see that they went after the gifts that made them feel good and look good, not the gifts that helped them be good and do good.

The Corinthian church loved the spiritual gifts that brought them a personal thrill or gave them a reputation in the community. It is easy to be more enamored with the gifts of the Spirit than the fruit of the Spirit. Galatians tells us that "when the Holy Spirit controls our lives, he will produce this kind of fruit in us: love, joy, peace, patience, kindness, goodness, faithfulness, gentleness, and self-control" (Galatians 5:22-23). Charisma can often win over character. We need agape love to help us keep our spiritual gifts in perspective. If we love God first, we will be more excited about the

Lord of the work than the work of the Lord. It's possible to love what we do in the church more than anything or anyone else. That's what the Corinthian church needed to understand—hence, Paul's description of love in chapter 13. It was necessary that Paul explain to them how agape love looks. God's love is interested primarily not in making *him* feel good but in blessing the objects of his love.

"WHAT DID YOU BRING US, DADDY?"

When we served a mission agency, Stuart used to travel for weeks on end. I always took the children down to meet him at Manchester airport when he returned from a trip. The children were small, and they would wait impatiently to see their father. Sometimes he had been away for three months. As soon as he came through customs, they would take off running toward him shouting, "Daddy, Daddy!" Their first question was always, "What did you bring us?" Sweet and childish? Yes! But very normal. Now they are grown, however, and we expect them to be more interested in the giver than the gifts (fortunately, they are!).

Are we? Is the Giver our focus, or do we pay more attention to our own (and others') gifts? All our loves—including love of the church and church work and love of our spiritual gifts—must be submitted to agape. That selfless love makes sure that God always stays more important than the gifts he gives us. In addition, loving people first, not what we are doing for them, is of prime importance.

Paul begins his description of love with an acknowledgment of the church's giftedness. But he says that their gifts are not being exercised in love. He says in essence, "You talk a lot, you know a lot, you give a lot, you work a lot—but you don't love a lot! If you don't love a lot, you are not a lot of good," or to quote him exactly, "No good to anybody" (1 Corinthians 13:2). In fact, Paul continues, "If I gave everything I have to the poor and even sacrificed my body, I could boast about it; but if I didn't love others, I would be of no value whatsoever" (1 Corinthians 13:3).

When I read these words, I need to sit my soul down and ask it some searching questions! "Soul, am I just making a big noise (like a clanging symbol)? Do I have a big head (boasting about my gifts)?" If so, then everything I am doing is no good to anybody and of no value whatsoever.

Ask yourself, *How much do I love the people I am working with, trying to reach or lead?* What is your attitude? Have you become so absorbed with your teaching, your singing, your training, or your doing that you can't see the people you are doing it for? Have you even lost sight of God?

You see, we can't fool people. Unbelievers can see childish behavior a mile away. And when people outside the church see behavior like this, they are often turned off. "Hypocrites, a bunch of hypocrites!" they charge. Unfortunately, they may be right.

Having Spiritual Gifts Doesn't Mean I'm Spiritual
How then do we put our gifts under agape's control? Paul was one of the most gifted people in the early church, but he had a healthy perspective on it all.

Take the gift of speaking in tongues, for instance. Paul told the Corinthians that all gifts were given for the good of the body as a whole. God gifted different people with different gifts to build everyone up, to help them be better Jesus lovers and glory givers. Paul himself had the gift of speaking in tongues, but *agape* controlled all his gifts. He was always asking the question, "What use of my gift will benefit the people the most?"

If it would confuse a visitor who had just come into the church meeting, Paul would restrain himself from using the gift of tongues in the assembly and speak instead in a way that the stranger would understand. He may have personally enjoyed speaking in tongues, but he was primarily concerned with the well-being of the visitor rather than his own. That's submitting his gift to agape.

God is concerned with our motives. He wants to see what is in our hearts. Are we motivated by love? Or are we motivated by money, fame, or fortune? Why are we doing what we are doing? What is the inside story? God is always more interested in *how* we are doing than in *what* we are doing. If we are interested in building only our little empire instead of the kingdom of God, it will show, and the world will have its worst suspicions confirmed. The world watches the church of Jesus Christ and sees too much that mirrors itself. Why, then, would they want to join us? After all, what's so different?

One of the youngsters that night at the fairground told me his reasons for not wanting to go to church. "It's the futility of the exercise," he said. I asked him to explain that to me.

"Well," he recounted, "I decided to go to church once, just to see what it was like. So I went, but as I got nearer, I noticed everyone was dressed up and I was in my jeans. So I thought I would sit outside and watch everyone who went in, hang around, and then watch everyone when they came out to see if it made any difference!"

"What did you see?" I asked, knowing the answer before it came.

"Everyone looked exactly the same," he answered. "So what was the point of going?"

What was the point, indeed! I don't think we are aware of the eyes that are watching us. But then, if we are self-absorbed, only interested in our own little Christian world, we won't care. Nothing puts off a world watching the church more than pride and self-absorption among its members. Humility, on the other hand, is very attractive to the outsider. Jesus, of course, is the best example.

Jesus was born in a stable, down a back alley, in obscurity. He could have arrived in a fiery chariot drawn by angels and accompanied by the host of heaven! He lived in Nazareth instead of Jerusalem, was a humble breadwinner for his family, and went around giving his life away. He healed people and told some of them not to tell about it! That's a far cry from how we use God's gifts.

> *Pride is so busy blowing his own trumpet,*
> *He's in danger of splitting the sides of his soul.*
> *Humility doesn't have a trumpet,*
> *He's a poor man*
> *Who came to make many rich!*
>
> —Jill Briscoe

Jesus told us to live lives of self-giving love and sacrifice. He modeled it for us. He told us to do our work humbly and quietly, without fanfare or ostentation. He said we should not let our right hand know what our left hand is doing. He instructed us to be satisfied with his "well done" at the end of the day instead of looking for praise from people. How have we gotten so far away from this sort of living?

Jesus kept his perspective because he stayed dependent on the Father. "By myself I can do nothing. . . . I seek not to please myself but him who sent me" (John 5:30, NIV). He wants us to be God-centered, not self-centered, and that must include our attitude toward our gifts, our church work, and our fellow believers.

So where do we begin? By beginning where we are. Have we discovered our gifts? Are we exercising them in the body of Christ with the right motives and the right attitudes?

What are your particular gifts of the Spirit? If you have been given up-front gifts, gifts that are very visible to others, you may be even more vulnerable to abusing them and grieving the Spirit who gave them to you! Can God trust you with up-front gifts? Can he rely on you not to let success go to your head? If not, you need to let God deal with some pride issues in your life.

THE PROBLEM OF PRIDE

Paul talks about a few of the spiritual gifts God had given to the church in Corinth in the chapters following 1 Corinthians 13. He talks about the gifts of speaking in tongues, prophesy, knowledge, faith, and giving. This is not an exhaustive list of the gifts of the Spirit. Rather, Paul was using these as examples of certain gifts that can get out of hand because they are up-front gifts and are therefore susceptible to pride.

I wonder if he mentions these particular gifts as examples because he knew that people need an awful lot of character to handle being so gifted. Think about it. Whom do we revere? People who appear spiritual, people who are really brainy and knowledgeable, the good speakers, people who show great faith, or those who give a lot of money. People with these gifts face more temptations than those who have less visible gifts. The Bible warns that "much is required from those to whom much is given" (Luke 12:48). It is often easy to be drawn off track when we are out there on the front lines.

Satan knows this, of course. He also knows that if he can cause a prominent gifted person to fall, either man or woman, he motivates more and more people, like my father, to swear they will never darken the doors of a church again.

As Stuart and I began to be invited to do some pretty up-front things in the church of Jesus Christ, my husband said to me, "We must always keep ourselves in perspective, Jill. One way we can do that is never to take ourselves too seriously!" That's why we have tried to see the ridiculous side of the things we do, tease each other a lot (different from putting each other down), and be accountable to lots of people. We need to ask God to help us see ourselves first as he sees us, and then as others see us. To paraphrase Scottish poet Robbie Burns: "Oh that God the gift would give us, to see ourselves as others see us!"

Paul says that if we are gifted, we are not to boast about it. Love doesn't boast. It always keeps things in perspective. We speakers are, after all, just a bunch of bleating sheep! Love "does not boast, it is not proud" (1 Corinthians 13:4, NIV). Above all, the thing that will keep our head the right size is an all-consuming love for God and others. Love isn't an old windbag. Who wants to hang around people whose conversations consist of "I, me, my, and mine"?

Kids talk like that, of course. Listen in on children's conversations, and that is all you will hear. But we are not to be little people but rather big people. I listened to a lady talking nonstop to a group of weary listeners the other day. She talked about "my church, my Bible study, my quiet time, and my short-term missions trip." Pride has to talk all the time and can't understand why everyone isn't interested. But love isn't full of its own importance. Love wants to know how other people like *their* church, if they are enjoying *their* Bible study, if *their* quiet time is productive for them, and asks to see the photos from *their* missions trip.

Lewis Smedes says:

> Boasting is a way of trying to look good when we suspect
> we are not good. Arrogance is an anxious grasp for power

when we fear that we are weak. Rudeness is putting people down in order to try to hold ourselves up. All three result from a loss of balance that comes when we are empty at the center. (*Love Within Limits*, 31)

When love for God is the central force in our lives, we are not empty at the center. Love counteracts our sinful natures that can so easily be proud, arrogant, and rude.

Empty trucks make the most noise. Boasting is our own little private campaign to publicize an image of ourselves. Pride doesn't listen with an eager mind, excited to be in church whoever is preaching. Pride is too eager to rate God's messenger. Pride is spending all its time imagining what it would do with this passage of Scripture if it were in the pulpit. It says, "I can do this for God, and I can do it better than anyone else!" You'll never find pride praying for grace, asking for strength, or pleading for mercy.

Jesus both modeled humility and told stories about it. He told a parable about a Pharisee and a tax collector who went into the temple to pray. The Pharisee looked up to heaven—where he was sure he was appreciated—and prayed, "I thank you, God, that I am not a sinner like everyone else, especially like that tax collector over there" (Luke 18:11). Meanwhile, the tax collector would not even lift up his eyes to heaven, but beat his breast and prayed, "O God, be merciful to me, for I am a sinner" (Luke 18:13). Jesus said the tax collector went home with a load lifted off his heart. He was justified before God. The Pharisee had spent his time trying to justify himself, which, of course, is useless.

I used to point a proud finger at the Pharisee. I have learned instead to watch for the Pharisee in me!

> *One day I found within my heart*
> *Someone who'd been there from the start,*
> *A prudish person self-appointed,*
> *Self-sufficient, self-anointed.*
> *Though I, a true disciple be*
> *I've met the Pharisee in me!*
>
> —Jill Briscoe

Do others see the Pharisee in me? Do they see me bragging about my gifts, showing off, doing without caring? I certainly hope not, for if they do, they will surely not be joining my church!

Bragging is a vocalizing of an inner arrogance. Paul says that love "does not boast, it is not proud" (1 Corinthians 13:4, NIV). Love doesn't vaunt itself. It isn't showy. It can serve without having to be appreciated or thanked.

When we submit our gifts to agape love, we can be used of God without others having to know about it. Have you ever led someone to Christ? Or maybe you have been used to encourage another along the way? Think back to the event. Did you share the incident with anyone? Why? Did you need someone to know how you had been used of God? Such information can even be "humbly" shared at a prayer meeting! This is immature behavior; it is not using our gifts with agape love. Children talk incessantly about themselves; adults should know better.

LEARNING HUMILITY

Pride always has to take the credit for a job well done, a victory achieved, a soul saved, a Christian helped. Pride always has to take the credit and never takes the blame. If something goes wrong, it is always someone else's fault. Pride would rather choke than say, "I'm sorry." Yet we can achieve so much more as long as we don't have to take the credit!

So how can we deal with our tendency toward pride and arrogance? How can we learn to let agape love rule our service and relationships in the church?

Spend Lots of Time in Worship

Isaiah looked through the doorway of heaven one day and saw the Lord high and lifted up, sitting on a throne. "Woe is me, for I am undone! Because I am a man of unclean lips, and I dwell in the midst of a people of unclean lips; for my eyes have seen the King, the Lord of Hosts" (Isaiah 6:5, NKJV). The best way for us to stop saying,

"Wow is me!" is to spend lots of time seeing the Lord who is high and holy. Then we will find ourselves saying, "Woe is me."

I was intrigued to hear Isaiah talk about his lips as being "unclean." To me, he is the golden-lipped prophet! Yet as he worshiped, he felt dirty and in need of cleansing.

Spend time with God. See the Lord high and lifted up, glorious and holy. If that doesn't cure your pride, nothing will!

Listen to Yourself, Look at Yourself

Listen to yourself talk, and then stop talking when it's all about you. Ask lots of questions about other people. Stop talking about your kids and ask about theirs. If there are single people in the group, remember that they have a family, too! Ask them to share their photos.

Use the Bible as a mirror of your soul. James says, "For if you just listen and don't obey, it is like looking at your face in a mirror but doing nothing to improve your appearance. You see yourself, walk away, and forget what you look like" (James 1:23-24). Look into God's Word and see yourself clearly. See the blemishes, but don't walk away and forget. Try to improve things you see in "the mirror."

Years ago I took care of our three-month-old grandson, Drew, for a day. The baby was upset much of the time, and I found it difficult to keep him happy. At last I found the answer. I held him up in front of the mirror in my bedroom. This worked wonderfully! Drew saw himself and cooed and talked to the mirror until his parents came back. I told Judy about it, explaining that as long as he saw himself, he was quite happy.

"Oh, Mom," my daughter replied, "he is at the age where he doesn't recognize himself. He thought it was another baby!" My daughter is a psychologist, so far be it from me to argue with her! But the incident gave me a good illustration. Like Drew, we look into the perfect law of liberty, the Word of God, and see ourselves reflected there with all our blemishes. Most of us don't really realize that we are seeing *ourselves,* and so we go away and do nothing about what we have seen. If we can allow God to show us our pride and arrogance, our rudeness and selfishness, and ask him to change us into his image, then the mirror will have done its good work in our hearts.

So listen to yourself and look at yourself. Then fix the blemishes you notice!

Humble Yourself

If we don't humble ourselves, then God will humble us! So dare to invite God to keep you humble. Now let me tell you this is an exceedingly dangerous prayer to pray! I have learned from experience what it's like to have God humble me—and it's not always a pretty picture! Yet I still dare to ask God to do what it takes to keep my head the size it should be, and he still delights to oblige. The Bible says, "Humble yourselves under the mighty power of God" (1 Peter 5:6), and I would add, "You had better do it, or God will do it for you!"

LOVING THE FLOCK

How does all this help us to love the people in the church? Well, Paul says, love will squelch the spirit of competition, stop the backbiting, and silence the slander—things about the church that turn more and more people off. Love is humble, and that is a virtue that our world strangely appreciates (perhaps because it sees it so seldom).

Paul took the Corinthians to task for taking sides. There were three great preachers around—Paul, Apollos, and Peter. Different groups chose their favorite and then the groups argued with each other about which preacher was the best. They compared them to each other, created a spirit of competition, and caused great dissension in the church. And all of the preachers had humbly presented the gospel of Jesus Christ! These preachers thought nothing of themselves. They were servants, but the people tried to set them up as heroes.

We are such "hero makers" today. We follow the lives of our "Christian stars," avidly reading everything about them. We compare teacher with teacher, saying one is better than the other. We join classes and insist that ours is the best leader instead of appreciating each unique gift. If each of us would humbly consider others as better than ourselves as we are told to do (Philippians 2:3), then there would be a sweet respect for everyone, and the world would see a huge difference.

Ask the Lord to help you to look at people with agape love, to look at them as he looks at them. Wish the best for them as you talk with them, ask them if you can pray for them. Learn to accept your fellow Christians as God's gifts to you, whoever they are. Actually, sometimes it is easier to love those outside the church than those inside! For example, what do I do with the awkward person who is always turning up on my committee making trouble for me?

Years ago, when we started neighborhood groups in our church, some of the congregation asked, "How are we going to determine who goes into which home group?" My husband explained that it would be decided by neighborhoods. But many people responded angrily, "Don't you tell me who my friends have to be!"

"I'm not," answered my husband. "I'm telling you who your sisters and brothers are in your subdivision!"

The groups were started, and soon the honeymoon wore off, and the hard job of loving the neighbors began. Just as we can't choose our blood relatives, we can't choose our church relatives! You see, we have two families—our own and the church family. Just as the family is the greatest place to work out loving relationships, so is the church family ideal for the job. What's more, we will be with them all in heaven, so we may as well learn to love and enjoy them down here.

Sometimes the Lord will use the strangest circumstances to put us together with people that we need practice loving. I do have a right to choose who my friends are, but not the right to tell God who my sisters and brothers in him will be. That is his business, not mine. His to choose them, mine to love them. Of course, it doesn't always work out that we end up loving (or even liking) everyone we work with in the church, but God intends for us to do a whole lot better than we have been doing! He intends for us to love with *his* love—agape love. He has given us his Holy Spirit and told us that "God has poured out his love into our hearts" (Romans 5:5, NIV). Our job is to learn to use all that available love to love the church!

Why is it so important to love the church? Because love opens people up to God. Love listens! Love learns! Love loves! People know if you love them; they know if you don't. When we were working with unchurched youth, we had no expertise, training, or even gifts that we were aware of for this work. We simply took off to places where unchurched kids hung out—the coffee bars and drug dives of the 1960s—and tried to get to know the people there. We invited them back to our home. This was proof that we were truly interested in them. They loved to come into our home. We listened. We tried to earn their trust so they would share their hearts with us. Those of us who really loved them were the first to hear their hearts! Those who were just fulfilling an outreach assignment from school didn't last long. They didn't love the kids, and the kids knew it. I asked that God would give me his love for these young people. He did, and they knew it. Love makes a bridge into someone else's life, and then God can use it as a highway into their hearts.

LOVE IS NOT AN OPTION

Years later I found myself in the United States of America. I was asked to work with women. I didn't like women; I liked kids. However, out of duty, I complied. I taught a Bible study and began to organize a women's ministry and saw them both grow. One day a friend of mine pulled me aside and said, "You are very good at what you do. You have a lot of shepherding gifts, but you do not love these women!" Ouch! She had caught me. She was right. I knew it, and I felt humiliated that apparently the flock knew it too.

So what should I do about it? I wondered. I could continue doing this job efficiently, all the while waiting for someone who had the "gift" of love to come along and love them. Or I could come to terms with the fact that love is not an option but a necessity! Jesus commanded that we love one another, so I needed to obey. If my gifts in women's ministry were to amount to more than a hill of beans, I needed to do what I had done years ago when I worked with youth: Ask God for the love I was incapable of myself. So I asked, and he gave. I look back on thirty years of women's ministry with joy. I could never have done it if I had not submitted my poor human love to Agape's control. He fueled my love for women all these years.

Who are you trying to love in the church? Are you coming up short? Submit your human love to Agape, and watch him transform it into a life-changing agent in other people's lives!

MAKING IT MINE

These questions can be used for personal quiet time or adapted for group discussions. A notebook, a Bible, and a pencil would be useful.

Thinking It Over

1. Think about these statements. Which strikes at your heart and why? *(a)* I have a bad case of "flock shock." *(b)* Spiritual gifts are tools, not toys. *(c)* Having spiritual gifts does not mean I am a spiritual person. *(d)* Love is not an option.
2. Share or journal about an experience with the church that could be described as "flock shock."
3. Define pride. What are some of its characteristics in the church? How can we develop humility?
4. Read Philippians 2.
   (a) Make a list of the ways Jesus humbled himself.
   (b) Make a list of the ways you can humble yourself.

Praying It In

1. Pray for your church—its leaders and its followers.
2. Pray for the people who have been turned off by the church for whatever reason.
3. Pray for yourself and how you can humbly use your gifts in your church.

Prayer

Oh, Lord, help me to stop playing games. Help me to listen to myself talk. Show me the way to recognize self-talk. Shut my mouth, Lord. If you could keep the lions' mouths closed in the den with Daniel, you can surely keep mine closed! Melt my heart; make it like yours. Let your agape love loose in and through my life. Let it show. This way people will honor you and sinners will be converted.

Bless my church, Lord. Use all the gifted people in it to exercise their gifts in love. Then the lost will beat a path to our door because so many people are looking for someone to love them. May they not be disappointed! May they say of our flock, "See how these Christians love one another." Thank you, Lord! Amen.

Living It Out

1. Decide to reevaluate your churchgoing. What can you do to really show your love for your church?
2. Reestablish contact with the church and the people in it.
3. Seek out people you are at odds with, and try to start again.

CHAPTER FOUR

LOVING THOSE WHO DRIVE US UP THE WALL

Be completely humble and gentle; be patient,
bearing with one another in love.
EPHESIANS 4:2 (NIV)

PAUL WRITES, "LOVE IS PATIENT AND KIND" (I CORINTHIANS 13:4). Most of us find that we can love those who are easy to love, but what about those who are hard to love or those who drive us up the wall (like your mother-in-law for instance)? I used to laugh at mother-in-law jokes until I became one. Then I entered a whole new world and found this traditionally hard relationship a challenge!

A CASE OF UN-LOVE

"My mother-in-law is coming to stay," a wide-eyed young woman told me. I noted the panic in her voice.

"Oh, really?" I answered. "That's nice."

"No it isn't," she replied. "We don't get along."

"Oh dear," I said.

"Do you think that's a terrible thing to say?" she asked. "After all, I'm a Christian, and she's a Christian. You'd think that would be enough."

I thought back to my relationship with my own mother-in-law. "No," I replied. "To be perfectly honest, I found my own relationship with my mother-in-law difficult too!"

She stared at me. "But you are a prominent Christian leader!"

"So? I am just a learner like everyone else in the matter of loving people. I have difficult people in my life just like you do in yours. What's more, I'm a difficult person too!"

"You are?" she gasped.

"Sure."

"What did you do to make things better?"

"I was content to have a peace-at-any-price policy," I answered, "until I got convicted one day when I was speaking. I was teaching on loving others, and it was just as if the Lord was standing at the podium by my side saying, 'Oh, just listen to you! You should try practicing what you preach!' A picture of my mother-in-law's face popped into my head, and I knew I had to address the issue. It was a classic case of un-love."

"What's that?"

"It's the opposite of much-love."

"Is it hatred?"

"No, not really. It's sort of neutral. It's a mutual tolerance between two people, a sort of silent agreement that there won't be any outright warfare, but there won't be any active loving either. You have to at least tolerate each other because you married into the family."

"I know exactly what you mean. It feels awful, though. I get sick to my stomach."

"Of course you do. It takes one of you to break the deadlock and take a risk."

"What do you mean?"

"One of you has to decide you've had enough and start to love the other one."

"I've tried, but I can't," she said quickly.

"Well, I know you can't on your own; for this you need Jesus," I said. I knew the young woman had Jesus, so I knew it was possible. "He loves everyone, even mothers-in-law. He can even love your mother-in-law through you!"

FROM UN-LOVE TO MUCH-LOVE

Our daughter, Judy, and I have a seminar we teach together on the story of Ruth and Naomi. I tell the story of what happened when my mother-in-law came to stay with us in America for three months and while here discovered that she had cancer.

Up to that point in our relationship, I had had no intention of anything more than a truce between us for the holidays. Certainly I had no plans to love her as God wanted me to, not that visit anyway. However, the discovery of her cancer changed everything. As Mother stayed with us in America and began to undergo treatment, I knew God had to do a deep, radical work in my life if I was to be able to nurse her to the end.

I went to talk to our family doctor, who was a wonderful Christian. I was honest with him. "Try as I might, I don't want her to stay with us," I blurted out. "I can't love her enough!"

He commended me for at least being honest about my fears of what was ahead, but he also challenged me to go for it and trust God. So I went home, got on my knees, and committed myself to the task.

Mother was having the same qualms about staying with us, and she was certainly wondering about me! She knew the limits I had placed on the boundaries of my love. We both threw ourselves on the Lord and prayed for a miracle! Over the terrible last eighteen months before she went home to England to die, God did what he does best. Agape love got control of my pathetic attempts to love her, fueling my human love until it burned brighter than I had ever dreamed possible. He worked the same miracle in Mother's heart. In the end she said, "Thank you, Jill. You have taught me how to live."

And I said, "Dear Mother, you have taught me how to die!"

It was done. God did it. There was no other way it could have happened. We had to have Jesus, and we did!

I shared this story with the young daughter-in-law who so feared her mother-in-law's visit. She cried. Then through her tears she said softly, "I'll do it!" Together we prayed for a miracle—a miracle that would start with her decision to love. After all, love is a decision to be primarily concerned with the other's well-being, irrespective of the person's attitude or reaction. Such love never fails. As we get to work, God takes our un-love and turns it into much-love!

Loving people when things are good between you is a whole different ball game from loving people when things are bad. Tough times in relationships come to all of us and indicate the caliber of our relationship with God and the extent of our love for him. We need to learn how to love even those who drive us crazy.

LOVING WHEN YOUR HEART IS BROKEN

We have been told to love, for love is not an option. We have been given by the Spirit the ability to love with agape love. Patience is another name for love, for Paul explained that "love is patient." Therefore, as we work through our difficult relationships, we will need to be patient. The meaning of the word *patience* (in Greek, *macrothumea*) is "long-suffering" or "slow to anger." Love suffers because it is the nature of love to suffer. Remember what C. S. Lewis said: "Love anything, and your heart will certainly be wrung and possibly be broken!" (*The Four Loves,* 169). But there is no alternative. We are not only *called* to love, we are also *commanded* to love.

Such love means loving not only when your heart is whole, but loving when your heart is broken. It means loving when the person you are trying to love is continuously hurting you afresh. Long-suffering means that love suffers well. Being inordinately fond of myself, I don't "do" pain very well. In fact, I don't do pain at all if I can help it! Do you? Who's for pain? The whole ethos of our society, as C. S. Lewis said, is to "embrace pleasure and eschew pain." It takes a radical act of God in our lives to so change our hearts that we are willing to embrace pain and eschew pleasure—to suffer for the sake of love! Yet, if that's what it takes to love someone, it must be done.

Patience is love waiting out a suffering situation. If pain cannot be avoided, then pain must be accepted. What we need to do is go with the pain and allow the pain to drive us to God.

> Don't waste the pain, let it prove thee.
> Don't stop the tears, let them cleanse thee.
> Rest, stop the striving, soon you'll be arriving in his arms.
> Don't waste the pain, let it drive you

Deeper into God.
He's waiting—and you should have come sooner!

—Jill Briscoe

Let pain drive you toward God and not away from him! Once you are deeper into God, you will find a bigger capacity to love even those who cause you pain.

God is very good at loving people who hurt him and are very hard to love. When Jesus was frustrated with the disciples one time, he said to them, "How long must I suffer you?" (Matthew 17:17, KJV). He then went on "suffering" them for a considerable time because he knew that this was God's will for him and he willed to do God's will. Long-suffering means being patient with an insufferable situation or person—even when you are hurting badly yourself—because it is the will of God. It hurts terribly to love at times like that, but that is what agape love does.

So how patient is God with people? The Old Testament tells us that "the Lord observed the extent of the people's wickedness, and he saw that all their thoughts were consistently and totally evil. So the Lord was sorry he had ever made them. It broke his heart" (Genesis 6:5-6). Fortunately, he didn't wipe the entire race off the map immediately, but first he patiently waited for people to repent. Noah, who had found grace in his eyes, preached forgiveness while building the ark. The New Testament, referring to this incident, says that "God waited patiently while Noah was building his boat" (1 Peter 3:20). God is surely patient! In fact, he waited 120 years and prepared a way for anyone sorry for his or her sin to find his grace and forgiveness.

In London there is a famous place called Hyde Park Corner. Anyone can get up on a soapbox there and talk about anything. Crowds usually gather to listen and to heckle. It is all pretty humorous, whatever the subject—politics, religion, and sex are favorites.

One day a famous preacher named Theodore Packer was preaching. He had his say through good-humored heckling, and then it was the turn of an atheist to give an opposing argument. That meant it was Theodore's turn to heckle. The unbeliever waxed strong and at one point, as he was finishing up blaspheming God, he shook his fist at heaven and said, "God, if you're there, I give you five minutes to strike me dead for what I have been saying about you!"

Theodore Packer spoke up, "Does the gentleman think he can exhaust the patience of God in five minutes?"

How long does your patience last? Does it last 120 years, 120 minutes, or 120 seconds? To have the patience God wants us to have, we need Jesus.

Love waits well! Don't you just hate that? I hate waiting for anything, especially for a circumstance to change or a person to say she is sorry. Patience loves on to give time for God's redemptive power to do its work. Love gives us the power to suffer long when we desperately want things to change.

ON THE WAY TO "SOON"

It takes spiritual maturity to be patient. Are kids patient? No! Will they wait? Not without a lot of fuss and bother! But Paul says we are to put away those childish ways and act like adults.

I was trying to comfort our three-year-old grandchild, who was howling because her daddy had kissed her good-bye and was on his way to work.

"He'll be back soon," I shouted soothingly. (It's hard to shout soothingly above a toddler's screams, but it can be done.) My best efforts, however, did not alleviate the pain of parting. I realized at once how stupid my attempt had been. After all, what does "soon" mean to a three-year-old child? When one is a toddler who loves her daddy very much, comfort is when "soon" turns to "now."

Waiting is not my favorite thing to do either. I've discovered that it's just the same for me as for small children. Like my grandchildren, I have real trouble with "soon." Especially when I have waited for something extremely important like a child to be conceived, a teenager to give just one little hint she liked belonging to me, or a relative to come to Christ. But no one knows how quickly "soon" will be. God knows, but he doesn't tell. His knowledge is withheld not to tease but to test!

Have you ever taken small children on a journey? What is their first question? "Are we nearly there?" That is pretty childlike. Yet how many times God has taken me on a dark and difficult journey and heard my childish query, "Father, are we nearly there?"— "there" being the end of the nightmare or the frustrating situation. Yet it is in the waiting that my patience grows!

Waiting for "closure" always exposes the real caliber of my faith. And when I'm waiting for some particular something to be over, there's bound to be some well-meaning saint who, lovingly and often with satisfaction, comes around to tell me how much deeper I will be when I am finished! I want to scream, "I don't want to be deeper. I want to stay shallow and have the hurt go away!" I've learned, however, that what you do with the waiting period is vitally important.

Waiting does not necessarily mean passivity. Waiting works us over, making us pliable in the Potter's hand. I'm learning to take action while I wait. On one particular plane ride, I found myself sitting next to a squirmy eight-year-old boy, and I learned some valuable lessons.

He settled back—for all of two minutes! He anxiously waited for liftoff, and after a few minutes of deep sighs and a lethargic attempt to read a comic book, he asked *the* question: "Are we nearly there?"

"I'm afraid not," I answered apologetically, feeling personally responsible for this vital piece of information. I hit a chord with him and made an eight-year-old friend. *Maybe no one has cared for his soul,* I mused. He was a little nervous, and I gently shared a bit about a God who keeps airplanes safe, who is interested in everyone, and who always listens to our prayers. Afterward, I thought about our conversation. Perhaps if we had arrived sooner, I wouldn't have gotten to know him. As he disappeared with the stewardess, I prayed for him and his salvation. While we are waiting, things can be accomplished that only God can do.

God's Waiting Room

Are you in God's waiting room? How is your patience? What are you waiting for? Are you waiting for a marriage to be mended or a mother to get well? Are you waiting for a misunderstanding to be rectified or a job to materialize? Perhaps you are waiting for someone to be released from his or her pain and suffering.

Years ago I watched my own mother fight with cancer to the death. I cried out in agony, "Lord, release her *now!*"

"Soon," he replied. And two days before she died she put her trust in Jesus. I am so glad he said "soon" and not "now."

Another time my husband called to tell me he was extending his evangelistic tour. "But it will soon be over," he assured me. His absence afforded me the extra waiting time to join a mission team and catch a big fish!

Waiting on the Lord does not mean waiting on everything else in life until the prayer is answered, the situation is fixed, or the nightmare is over. Waiting on the Lord gives us a chance to grow trust while we busy ourselves with whatever personal responsibilities we have.

The devil loves to slow us to a dead stop, telling us we need to wait until things are okay again before we can serve, teach, preach, or take up our daily duties. He would paralyze us with the pain of waiting. The devil says, "Wait until things are normal." God says, "Keep working while you're waiting."

Next time a problem arises in your life and you are tempted to ask, "Are we nearly there?" settle in for the long haul and learn patience. How can we learn it unless God gives us a reason to use it?

It is hard to be in God's waiting room, but love accepts a difficult situation without giving God a deadline to remove it. God wants to see us grow patience and trust in the soil of our suffering.

Waiting on the Rooftop

Perhaps you are waiting and watching like the father of the Prodigal. You are up on the rooftop, straining your eyes for a glimpse of a returning prodigal. How hard it is to watch and pray! Ruth Bell Graham is a favorite poet of mine. Not only does she write wonderful poems, but they come from the heart of her own experience. You may want to stop right now and borrow her prayer. Make it your own for your prodigal, and take heart.

Listen, Lord,
a mother's praying
low and quiet:
listen, please.
Listen what her tears
are saying,
see her heart
upon its knees;
lift the load
from her bowed shoulders
till she sees
and understands,
You, who hold
the worlds together,
hold her problems
in Your hands.

—*Prodigals and Those Who Love Them*

We need to patiently trust God to take care of our prodigals. That means to believe that he hears our prayers so we can safely leave the worrying to him.

I used to think trusting God meant trusting him to do what I wanted him to. I have come to realize that it means trusting him to do what *he* wants to. I am still struggling with situations I need to "wait out" in patience. I am struggling to trust him to hear and answer prayer in his own time and in his own way. The deadlines seem so urgent, but God's time is not our time. Will we relax and trust him to do what is best for everyone in the big picture? Patience and trust are sisters. Patience—gritting your teeth and bearing it—is a miserable affair. Trust makes a miserable affair a marvelous affair! Trust, like love, is a decision.

Waiting for God's Best

One of the hardest things to wait for is the right partner to come along. How much carnage has been caused because people couldn't wait for God to bring the right person into their lives. Love waits for God to bring the right person along or does without.

One of the best examples of this is the love story of Jacob and Rachel. Do you remember how the two met? Jacob had swindled his brother, Esau, out of his blessing and his birthright and had to leave home in a hurry. Esau, holding a grudge against his brother, let it be known that he would take revenge (Genesis 27:41). This became known to Rebekah, their mother, who advised Jacob to go to his Uncle Laban, who lived far away. He could lie low till his brother's wrath had diminished. So Jacob did what his mother suggested.

On the way, Jacob had an encounter with God and got his life back on track (Genesis 28:20-22). Laban gave him a job, and while Jacob was at Laban's place, he fell in love with Laban's beautiful daughter, Rachel.

Laban asked Jacob to work for him for seven years in order to gain Rachel's hand in marriage. Jacob did so, and Laban prospered under Jacob's tenure. Seven years seems a long time to wait for the woman you love, but when it is the right one, it seems as nothing. In fact, that was exactly what Jacob discovered. "Jacob spent the next seven years working to pay for Rachel. But his love for her was so strong that it seemed to him but a few days" (Genesis 29:20). Laban didn't want Jacob or his daughter to leave, so he thought up a plot to keep them with him after the wedding.

When it came to the wedding day, Laban cheated Jacob by giving him Leah, his oldest (and plainest) daughter, instead of the beautiful Rachel! Jacob didn't know until the morning, and then the Bible says simply, "It was Leah!" (Genesis 29:25). It beats me why he didn't know till the morning, but it probably had something to do with the coverings the bride wore and the fact that there was no electric light. After the shocking discovery, Laban told Jacob that if he wanted Rachel, he could have her, but he must work for him for seven more years. And Jacob did! Now there's love for you. When seven years seems like nothing because of the love you feel, and then you add seven more and it still seems like nothing, that's impressive! Jacob patiently waited out the time and kept faith with Laban (who had clearly cheated him) because he loved Rachel so much.

Can you wait for your "Rachel"? Will you wait out a frustrating situation, believing God loves you and wants the very best for you? Then stop giving him deadlines! Agape love is very patient. For this you need Jesus, but for this you have Jesus!

Patiently Doing the Right Thing
Being patient with kids is another real test of love. If patience is another name for love, then the parenting experience is ideal for producing it in us! How patient do you need to be with kids? And I don't mean being patient with any old thing; I mean patiently doing the right thing!

I love a quote by Susannah Wesley. Someone said to her, "I wonder at your patience. You have told that child twenty times the same thing." To which she replied, "If I had satisfied myself by only mentioning it nineteen times, I should have lost all my labor. It was the twentieth time that crowned it!" For this, Susannah Wesley needed Jesus, but for this she had Jesus.

I remember struggling with my temper when I was teaching preschool. Overcrowded classrooms in Liverpool led to pressure-cooker situations all day. Again and again I lost my patience with the kids. I would come home feeling absolutely miserable and throw myself on my knees saying, "Lord, I did it again! Forgive me!" I knew I needed patience beyond myself. I knew God was living in me and he was patient beyond measure, but I just didn't know how to connect his patience with my temper. Have you ever felt like that? And with this lack of self-control comes guilt. *How can I feel like this about my kids?* I scolded myself.

Then one day when I lost my patience one more time, I seemed to hear God say to me, "These children are awful today!" I couldn't believe my ears. He thought so too! That was the turning point. He was not standing in the corner of my classroom condemning me;

rather, he wanted me to know he was on my side agreeing with me. Then he reminded me that I had all it took to control myself—I had *him!* Those kids were pushing him to the limits, too, but he was perfectly in control of himself. I just needed to appropriate his power to be patient. I stopped what I was doing and threw myself on him. "Help, Lord, I can't do this alone. Give me the patience I need!" As I relaxed, the peace came at once, and with the peace, the patience.

I need to trust him for the rest of my life with this issue. Each time I feel myself losing it, I need to glance heavenward and shout, "Help!" The power comes as I exert my will to be lovingly firm and do the right thing.

KINDNESS IS PATIENCE IN ACTION

So is it passive—this love that is so patient with mothers-in-law, prodigals, and obnoxious kids? Well, there is an active part to it. Paul says that not only is love patient, it is also kind. Kindness is the active part of patience. Patience is *being* good, while kindness is *doing* good. Kindness is goodness showing. Love is kind to those who would do it harm. Jesus said that we are to love even our enemies. To do that, we definitely need him!

Being Kind to Those Who Hurt Us
I think of an incredible example of such kindness in the life experience of Tania Rich, a young mother serving the Lord with her husband in the jungle. Read her story:

> January 31, 1993, was "just a regular day in the village.". . . Suddenly, Tania heard loud noises, gunshots and shouting. Guerillas had surrounded the village and had entered each of the three missionaries' homes. A gunman came into the bedroom where Tania was with the sleeping girls. She came out with him, and saw that Mark [her husband] was with two other guerillas who had him facedown, his hands tied behind his back. Mark shouted in Spanish for the gunman

to leave Tania alone and not harm her. The gunman approached Tania and demanded money, and she complied. Then he asked for coffee and sugar. In recalling the incident, Tania laughed, "When the gunman fumbled with the money and the packages of food, I found myself asking, 'Would you like a bag for that?' He just stared at me incredulously!" ("Waiting without Knowing . . . ," *Just Between Us,* spring 1996, 7)

Now there you have it! A practical act of love! Love does good to those who would do it harm. Tania found that what was inside of her—the love of Jesus—came out in a terrible time of crisis. She offered something to her husband's persecutors. (There were three missionary families living in the village, and the guerrillas took the three men. Sadly, the men were never found but were declared dead in 2001.) Tania loved the people she and Mark had gone to help find the Lord. When the big test came, she reacted out of that love in an astonishing act of kindness. Love does good to those who do it harm.

Think of Jesus. He healed his enemies (the servant of the high priest whose ear Peter severed in the Garden of Gethsemane) and prayed for the soldiers who were crucifying him: "Father, forgive these people, because they don't know what they are doing" (Luke 23:34). He taught his disciples, "Love your enemies! Pray for those who persecute you!" (Matthew 5:44). When others are being cruel, try being kind. When you are being given a hard time, think of a practical act of love to do in return. Ask, "What can I do for them?" not "What can I say to them?" or "What can I do to get back at them?"

Since the sad news has come that the three missionary men have been confirmed dead, the three women haven't missed a step. Now they have been able to bring closure to their unbelievable situation and get on with their lives. They have not lost their love for the tribes and their huge desire to reach them for Christ. That is because love suffers long and is kind. Love never fails to go on loving and giving, finding any way it can to win the lost.

Being Kind to Those Who Don't Deserve It

Let's bring this closer to home. Not too many of us are asked for such displays of endurance and courage. But many of us have teenagers. Those of us who have teenagers or have raised them know what a difficult stage this is.

Our daughter and I got into difficulties when she would not pick up her room. Try as I might to bully, threaten, or cajole, she would not clean it. The issue became a flash point. One day I was asking advice from a wise woman at church. "Just try being kind to her," she suggested.

"She doesn't deserve it!" I replied.

She smiled understandingly. "That's what kindness is for. Anyway, you have tried everything else, why not pick up her room for her and see if that will work?"

I had nothing to lose, so I did. Four days later there was no response, and I was just about to give up. Then my daughter burst into tears and said she was sorry. "What made you say you're sorry?" I asked curiously.

"You've been so kind to me, Mom," she replied.

It might not work for you, but in the face of such resistance to persuasion, being patiently kind when someone doesn't deserve it may actually get you somewhere. After all, "God's kindness leads you toward repentance" (Romans 2:4, NIV). So the kindness of God through you may lead others to repentance, too!

Kindness Is Servanthood

The words *kindness, goodness,* and *gentleness* are all closely allied. Another word for kindness is *servanthood.* Love is a servant. Just look at Jesus. Jesus washed feet. Would we?

I remember seeing a movie where a woman was being interviewed for a job. "I don't do windows," she said, to no one's surprise. I think the church is full of people like that. They call themselves servants, but they don't do windows, or they don't do feet!

Think about children. How much energy does it take to get them to do their chores? They don't do windows. The ability to serve to that degree comes with maturity, or it should. Children by nature are not kind and serving creatures. When I was a teacher in Liverpool in a pretty tough school in a tougher neighborhood, teachers were assigned playground duty. We used to call it "vice patrol." As I took my turns, I was amazed at how cruel those children could be to each other. I saw kids bullying little kids or excluding others or mercilessly teasing them till they were reduced to tears.

Servanthood means doing a practical loving act for someone who needs it—maybe visiting an elderly neighbor who is alone and cooking her a good meal, perhaps pitching in and cleaning up the kitchen after a women's meeting at church (even if you were the speaker!), or deliberately taking another turn in the nursery even if you've done your bit in the past.

Servanthood looks for a way to do the things that are menial. A servant takes out the trash or pours water in a bowl and washes feet (in Jesus' day this was the job of the lowest level of slaves). Servanthood is helpful all the time, looking to bless, heal, and encourage those less fortunate. Servanthood welcomes the opportunity to be a servant not only when it's voluntary but also when it's not an option.

Maybe some of us need to do some growing up in this area of servanthood. Growing up in the Lord and in his agape love means growing in patience and kindness. Agape love gives you the power to be patient and kind to all sorts of frustrating people. Love suffers all sorts of indignities. In fact, love suffers longer than you think you can. J. B. Phillips paraphrases I Corinthians 13:4: "This love of which I speak is slow to lose patience—it looks for a way of being constructive." That is another way of saying "Love is kind."

THE GIFT OF FRUSTRATION

It is important to recognize that any frustrating situation that requires patience is God's gift to you. A gift that, if received with the right attitude, will present the opportunity to spend some time in God's waiting room practicing patience. Hey, that's not all bad! Frustration is often God's way of driving us to him.

I was standing at a ticket counter in a large American city presenting my tickets for a missions trip to Europe. "There is a problem," the agent said. We then began a long irritating talk about all the things that were wrong with the itinerary, the tickets, and everything else, it seemed.

In vain I pointed out that I had spent six months making sure everything was right so that there would not be a problem. I could see that I was going to miss the plane and the first leg of the trip. Then who knew what would happen to the rest of the tickets? I felt my anxiety level rising. I prayed (briefly) and resumed the argument. How could this situation be a gift to me from God? Was it not rather from the devil? As if I was having a side conversation with God, I began to debate this with the Almighty while I argued with the girl.

"Lord," I said petulantly, "why is this happening? This girl is so irritated with me, and I am so irritated with her. Sort her out, Lord!"

"*You* sort her out, Jill," I distinctly heard him say! "And do it with grace, sweetness, and patience!" I didn't want to hear that. I wanted to have the girl's superior rebuke her, show her how right I was the whole time, and get me on that plane! Suddenly, I recognized what was happening. This situation was God's gift to me. It was a miniworkshop at the start of my day. For this I needed Jesus, but for this I had Jesus!

Perhaps I was the only Christian this girl had ever met. (Now that was a scary thought!) Drawing on the Spirit for grace and patience, I smiled at the girl. She looked at me in amazement. "Look," I said. "I'm sorry for my impatience. This is a very important trip, and I am getting really anxious. But I know you need to do your job. Is there some way we can find a quick solution?"

Without a word, she beckoned me through the door into her supervisor's office. The problem was solved, and I caught my plane!

You win half the battle already when you recognize the problem as a gift. It is a gift because these types of situations enable you to experience the love of God in a special way. People are receptive when they are struggling with frustration. If they are expecting others to act with frustration, they cave in if you exhibit kindness. If you can go beyond sounding kind to being kind and doing an outrageous act of kindness, this speaks louder than a thousand words. It can open people up to hear about the Lord. Think of Mother Teresa and how her practical acts of love on the streets of Calcutta spoke about the love of Christ to the dying and destitute.

Doug is a friend of ours who served as a missionary to India. He himself ended up in a tuberculosis hospital there. Even though he was really sick, he tried to give out literature to the other patients in the ward. No one was interested in what a "rich American" had to say, so they refused to accept his literature.

One night a little man opposite him struggled to get out of bed to go to the bathroom. He didn't make it. Everyone complained of the mess and the smell, but no nurse came to help him. The same thing happened the following night. Sick to his stomach and weakened by the disease, Doug dragged himself out of bed, picked up the little man who was in such distress, and carried him to the bathroom. There, Doug cleaned the man, carried him back to bed, and then made him a cup of tea. Exhausted with the effort, Doug collapsed back into his own bed.

The next day all the people in the ward accepted the literature Doug passed out to them! Of course they did. He had done an outrageous act of kindness, and it opened their hearts.

The parable of the Good Samaritan pictures such kindness. The Jews hated the Samaritans, but when a Samaritan found a Jew robbed and beaten and left for dead in a ditch, he got off his donkey to help him. He was amazingly kind to the man. That is the picture Jesus gives us of loving others with agape love.

Kindness is the active part of patience. Patience is being good and kindness is doing good. The helpful thing about doing good is that you don't have to wait till you feel like doing good to do it. Try doing it when you don't feel like it. Like the Samaritan, get off your high horse (or donkey), get down in the ditch, and bind up someone's broken heart with a practical act of kindness—doing things you don't need to do, things that no one expects you to do, the things that go far beyond the call of duty.

> *Kindness gets on his horse in the morning*
> *rides along with his eyes wide open.*
> *He sees the man in the ditch,*
> *and he stops to help.*
> *Kindness never worries if he will get hurt in the helping.*
> *He's too concerned for the sick one,*
> *the hurt one,*
> *and the dying one.*
> *He pours out his healing help into a poor man's wounds.*
> *He binds them up with grace,*
> *and he always goes out of his way.*
> *He'll be back!*
> *Back to check on the man's progress.*
> *Back to see if he can do anything more.*
> *Kindness is patiently insisting on getting his hands dirty,*
> *taking risks,*
> *loving strangers,*
> *getting poorer while others get richer.*
> *Kindness is always dying to do love!*
>
> —Jill Briscoe

In the end, it helps to meditate on the goodness and kindness of God. If you fasten your thoughts on him and how incredibly kind he is, your dark mood will lift. Try it and you'll see! Again Ruth Bell Graham offers those of us too down to look up a prayer without words.

> *Sunk in this gray*
> *depression*
> *I cannot pray.*
> *How can I give*
> *expression*
> *when there're no words*

to say?
This mass of vague
foreboding,
of aching care,
love with its
overloading
short-circuits prayer.
Then through this fog
of tiredness,
this nothingness, I find
only a quiet knowing
that He is kind.

—*Prodigals and Those Who Love Them*

Think often upon God's infinite kindness and see what will happen to your gray depression. Then go and find someone to be patient and kind to!

Is your love patient and kind? Remember, the Holy Spirit dwells in your hearts to be all the things you are not. Draw on this resource. Love that works, works at love. There is no other way.

MAKING IT MINE

These questions can be used for personal quiet time or adapted for group discussions. A notebook, a Bible, and a pencil would be useful.

Thinking It Over

1. Think about some definitions of patience and kindness. Which one helps you most and why?
2. Are you a patient person? Do you get discouraged in situations in which you have to wait patiently?
3. Fill in the acrostic on patience. Choose a word for each letter.

PAINFUL

A

T

I

E

N

C

E

4. Discuss or write a sentence about an outrageous act of kindness someone blessed you with. Spend some moments thinking about someone who needs you to bless them in kind. Ask God to give you an idea of what you could do.
5. Pick one of these phrases and write a letter to God about it, or discuss it with someone.
   (a) I want to stay shallow and have the hurt go away.
   (b) Comfort is when "soon" turns to "now."
   (c) God was sorry he had made us.
   (d) We need to get off our high horse and get in the ditch.
   (e) Kindness is always dying to love.

Praying It In

1. Pray for people who are
   - waiting
   - suffering patiently
   - being kind
   - in the ditch

2. Spend time being thankful for people who have loved you patiently and kindly.
3. Pray for the church, that people would be kind to strangers.

Living It Out

Take one idea from this chapter and plan an outrageous act of love and kindness for someone.

   - Who will that person be?
   - When will you do it? Decide on the day.
   - How will you start?
   - Will you ask someone to help you? Who will that person be?
   - Go for it!

CHAPTER FIVE

LOVING OTHER PEOPLE'S THINGS MORE THAN OUR OWN

Love . . . does not envy.
1 CORINTHIANS 13:4 (NIV)

WHEN I RAN A PRESCHOOL, I HAD AN OPPORTUNITY TO SEE envy up close, all day, every day. A child would pick up a doll and begin to play with it. Immediately another child would want that same toy. Then it began: "I want what you've got!" would develop into "If I can't have it, I don't want you to have it either!" A fight would ensue, whereupon I would intervene and attempt to sort it out. This was to be expected with three- and four-year-olds. I was hopeful that as the children grew, they would grow out of such behavior. Remember Paul's words? "When I grew up, I put away childish things" (1 Corinthians 13:11). We expect children to do the same, don't we?

Have we truly put childish ways behind us? How does our love rate? If we are loving with *agape* love, we do not envy others.

ONE OF THE BIG TEN

Love does not envy (or covet) for a number of reasons. First, because it breaks one of God's big ten—as in the Ten Commandments—and second, because we have all our heart needs met in our relationship with Christ. Coveting doesn't seem like such a big deal to us, yet it is one of God's "big" commands right there in Exodus 20:17: "Do not covet your neighbor's house. Do not covet your neighbor's wife, male or female servant, ox or donkey, or anything else your neighbor owns."

Just in case people don't understand God's instructions not to covet, he made a list for us right there in his command. Maybe he knew how we Westerners love lists! This is helpful. You are not to covet your neighbor's house or your neighbor's spouse. You are not to covet your neighbor's servants, your neighbor's ox or donkey, or anything that is your neighbor's. Now there you have it! Let's take them one at a time.

Your Neighbor's House

Have you ever looked next door or across the street and said, "I wish we had enough money to buy that house"? Or have you ever been invited out to dinner and spent the evening coveting practically everything you saw? Or perhaps it's not the house but where the house is! "If only we could move across town," you gripe, "then we could get away from these obnoxious neighbors! If only we had nice neighbors like our friends have, life would be better." When you lived in an apartment, did you want to live in a house? When you lived in a house, was it hard not to want a bigger one? When you rented, was it hard not to want to buy? There is no end to it, is there?

Your Neighbor's Spouse

Maybe you don't want to move an inch because you have fallen in love with your neighbor's husband or wife and suspect that your sentiments are returned. It could be you feel some chemistry between the two of you and, being somewhat tired or bored with your own marriage, have a growing excitement in your heart. You are flirting internally, thinking no one knows about it. Well, I have news for you: God knows about it and is not pleased. He knows where coveting of this kind could lead.

Your Neighbor's Servants

Perhaps you say, "I wish I had household help. If I only had someone to clean my house like my cousin does or someone to help me with the children even one day a week, I would be a better mom." It's a short step from that point to coveting your cousin's house help! Or maybe it is the "silent servants" you want. A fancier washing machine and dryer, a new dishwasher or refrigerator, or a fancy bread machine. I remember living at a youth center without a washer or dryer. We had three children under school age, and it was very hard to wash and dry everything by hand, especially in England when there was never a day when the sun shone so I could hang the clothes out to dry! I couldn't help gazing with longing at my mother's washing machine when I went to visit.

Your Neighbor's Ox or Donkey

The ox and donkey represent a person's business and mode of transportation. One of the most common things to envy is the vehicle someone has that we don't. "If only I had a new car instead of an old car," we say wistfully. Or, "Why can't my husband buy me a little sports car like my friend's husband bought her?" Or a problem arises in your heart because you are jealous of the promotion your husband's colleague received. It's just not fair!

Anything Else That Is Your Neighbor's

Just in case you think you have escaped, God's list ends with a comprehensive sentence that covers anything else you may covet. "Anything" includes clothes, jewelry, vacations, good looks, talents and abilities, nationality, athletic prowess, education, age, health—or anything else you can think of. You can covet your friend's opportunities to go to a better college than you, or you may even want your children chosen for the school play instead of more talented kids. Whatever anyone has can be coveted by someone else—and chances are, whatever you have is being coveted by someone. Envy leads to hatred, and hatred leads to all manner of evil. What a vicious and angry circle we all are in when we envy one another!

The word *envy* pictures a person seething and boiling over. All of us have experienced such an emotion. It is a petulance that comes from a pouting heart. It is hatred without a cause that destroys us from the inside out. It is not a little thing. Knowing the destructive power of envy, God has moved to help us. He has loved us with an everlasting love and wants our experience of this to so fill us up and satisfy us that there is no unsatisfied place left and no need for envy.

Coveting comes in all shapes and sizes. It tempts us at all ages and at all stages of our lives. Not all coveting leads to hatred, of course, but it can. It often brings disruption to our relationships, unimagined disaster, and damage to the most important relationship of all—our relationship with God. Whenever we break even one of his commandments, we displease him, do ourselves no good, and bring sorrow and grief to others. And it can all begin when we look longingly at something someone has that we don't.

We say, as my preschool child said when snatching the doll from another little girl's arms, "I want what you've got!" Then if we don't get it, we allow envy to deteriorate into deep bedrock jealousy that says, "And I don't want you to have it either!" Who knows where this will lead? Coveting is a sleeping lion. When we are awakened by the "greed need" within, things can get out of hand in a hurry and we may find ourselves planning and doing things we could never have imagined. Now that's a scary thought!

"If Only"

I was at a typical gathering of church women in an American city. I asked a leading question to get the women talking. "What would make you more content than you are at this present time? Start your answers with 'If only,' " I suggested.

"If only I could live in a bigger house," a middle-aged woman sighed. I could understand that. I remembered living in a really tiny house when Stuart and I were in youth ministry, and longing for more space. After all, the other youth workers seemed to have more space than we did, and they didn't need it as much as we did! There I was, wanting the space in my home that others had in theirs. After all, we were going to use it for ministry.

"If only I were as pretty as my sister," responded another woman. I could certainly relate to that! I grew up in the shadow of a stunning sister. I remembered how fed up I was with all the boys wanting to get to know me so they could get to know her!

"If only I had the chance to go to college," still another chipped in. "All my siblings got to go but me." I could understand. I never had the chance to go to Bible school.

"I'd be happy if I could go skiing with the family like my brother and his kids do instead of only being able to afford to go camping," added a young, upwardly mobile homemaker. Who of us has not grown envious hearing about the exotic vacations someone else takes!

"If only I had a husband and family, I'd be content never to go anywhere!" a single girl said softly. And so it went on. It seemed each woman was urged on by another's discontent.

I thought how easy it is to live our lives in the shadow of "if only."

But it is high time we realized that coveting is a sin! I realized that fact when I first read the Ten Commandments. There it was in black and white for all of us spoiled, discontented people to read. God has said loudly and clearly, "Do not covet." Every time we break that commandment, God says, "And what part of 'do not' do you not understand?" Even if we say "if only" silently in our hearts, God hears us loud and clear!

I grew up playing the "if only" game. Not growing up as a Christian, I had never read the Bible and didn't know how Jesus could satisfy me. I had this gnawing sense of discontent, and I assumed that it was because I had not found the person, thing, or situation that would satisfy me. So I played the "if only" game. It seemed I never got to the end of that game. If only I were as pretty as my sister; if only I were smaller and didn't tower over the boys; if only the war were over; if only I could be captain of the tennis team at school; if only a handsome Englishman would appear and carry me off so I could live happily ever after.

And then there was the more serious stuff: If only I could stop lying or cheating at exams or acting like a fool; if only I could clean up my act; if only I could find the reason for being; if only I could feel I was worth something! If only I could love people as much as I loved my selfish self. If only I could get to know my earthly father better. If only I could stop swearing. If only I could stop saying, "If only"! And if only I could stop the internal panic rising inside me day by day when I began to wonder what would happen if none of my "if onlys" ever happened.

And then I found Christ!

Now, many of my "if onlys" have been answered. The Son of God walked into my heart, and the day dawned! How could I have lived in so much darkness and never known it? The day dawned and the birds sang and my world was changed! In the words of an old hymn:

> *Heav'n above is softer blue,*
> *Earth around is sweeter green!*
> *Something lives in every hue*
> *Christless eyes have never seen:*
> *Birds with gladder songs o'erflow,*
> *Flow'rs with deeper beauties shine,*
> *Since I know, as now I know,*
> *I am His, and He is mine.*

Yet it wasn't long after I had come to faith and the first euphoria passed that I began to hear the urgent "if only" voices again. How could I still be saying, "If only"? I felt more guilt than I had ever felt before I became a Christian. Christians are not supposed to be unsatisfied. They are not supposed to envy other Christians who appear to have all their "if onlys" satisfied. What was wrong with me?

DON'T FEED THE CUCKOO

At that early stage in my Christian walk, I didn't know that my old nature had not been eradicated when I became a Christian. I didn't know it would be a lifetime battle to live in the Spirit and not give in to the deeds of the flesh—one of those deeds being to allow myself to be discontented. My success in that battle depended on which nature I was going to "feed"—my old covetous nature or my new spiritual nature.

There is a bird called the cuckoo. It is a big, lazy, and rather ugly bird. It is too lazy to build its own nest, so it flies around until it finds a nest that is already built. Then it lays a large egg in it. The smaller bird whose nest has been commandeered returns from looking for worms and doesn't notice that "things ain't like they used to be." So she does her best to hatch all the eggs, including the huge cuckoo's egg, and somehow manages it. Then she starts to try to feed her brood. Of course, the largest mouth gets the most worms and ends up tipping the little birds out of the nest and reigning supreme.

This is a great picture of the flesh and the spirit. There are two natures in us—the old nature and the new one. The nature we feed will reign supreme. If we insist on feeding the sinful covetous nature, then that will be the nature that gains the advantage. If we allow ourselves to play the "if only" game all day long, the old "cuckoo" will dominate our minds, our wills, and our actions. We feed the "cuckoo" when we set our desire on something that is unattainable, illegitimate, or simply not in the plan of God for our lives. If we dream, fantasize, and repeatedly feed our thoughts with images of the coveted object, we will starve the new nature and eventually spiritual desire will die.

How will I know if I am feeding the wrong nature? I will know if I have a chronic sense of discontent, a yearning for fulfillment that I have convinced myself I cannot have unless I possess the "if only."

WANTING MORE

Wanting what others have is a disease. What's more, it's catching! If you are around people who are never happy and are always grumbling, you'll find yourself infected with the same "grumble germ." Yet love is the medicine that cures the ailment.

Paul told the Corinthians that coveting was childish and dangerous behavior and they needed to grow out of it. He wrote, "Love is not jealous" (I Corinthians 13:4); "Love doesn't want what it doesn't have" (*The Message*). Love loves God supremely and one's neighbor as oneself. That is possible because we are satisfied with the Beloved alone.

Wanting More Money

"Keep your lives free from the love of money and be content with what you have." How can we do that? "Because God has said,

'Never will I leave you; never will I forsake you'" (Hebrews 13:5, NIV). The problem with many Christians is that they want Jesus *and* something else—as if Jesus isn't enough by himself. This internal yearning for something more needs to be addressed.

John the Baptist told the soldiers among the crowds that were coming to him for baptism, "Be content with your pay" (Luke 3:14). Now there's a novel thought! Is anyone ever content with his or her wages? So many of us are looking for something more—we just don't know how to be content.

You can envy anything or anyone. You can envy the person who is paid more than you are, the one who possesses more than you do, or the one who is appreciated more than you are. Coveting is all about *more*—more than I have, however much that is. One of the richest men in the world was asked, "How much is enough?" He replied, "Just a little bit more than I've got!" The poorest person as well as the richest person can be eaten up with envy.

Wanting More Gifts

Money isn't the only thing that is coveted; in fact, people can envy the strangest things. The Christians in the Corinthian church were actually envying each other's spiritual gifts! They wanted the showy gifts, the up-front gifts, the gifts that would get them noticed (for their spirituality!). Paul explained that they should not envy the more spectacular gifts but be content with the gifts they had been given, exercising them in a spirit of humility and thankfulness.

We have a real problem in the West today because we have gotten heroes mixed up with celebrities, even in the church. People with the "showy" gifts have been turned into Christian celebrities, sometimes overnight. A musician bursts onto the Christian circuit or someone writes a book or speaks at a big convention, and we begin to "hero worship," often doing a young musician or speaker a great disservice. This can even turn into a form of idolatry. This leads other people with some sort of up-front talent to covet the limelight and attention, too. It can cause a speaker in a small venue to want instead to be a speaker in a big venue.

Paul's words are very relevant for us today. Who are the Christian heroes we should be telling our children about? Consider the humble missionary or quiet servant of the Lord. Who is writing books about them? Who do we present on our church platforms? People working downtown in our rescue missions or the author of the latest best-seller? Paul tells us we should give attention to the people who work behind the scenes or who faithfully do a sterling job out of sight. The daughter who nurses her father in his last days, the young couple who adopts the handicapped child, the couple who stays married for fifty years! These are God's heroes. The Corinthians were getting celebrities and heroes mixed up just like we do, and this was leading to a lot of coveting.

Have you ever been discontent with your gifts and wanted what others have? "If only I could sing like she does!" or "If only I could lead the women's work in church." Or we may get fed up if we *only* have the gift of helping when we would rather have the gift of leadership and have someone help us instead! We must grow out of such childish behavior.

Since September 11 there has been a healthy shift in this regard. The first Halloween after the atrocities in Manhattan saw little children dressed as the new heroes of the hour. Costumes of firefighters and police officers were quickly sold out as children used the occasion to show what they thought of the brave men and women who gave their lives to help others. We can hope that our children had their attention brought to focus on how much better it is to save each other than to kill each other, to help each other than to hate each other, to love each other than to lynch each other.

But sadly, it didn't take too long to see the covetous nature within engulf the new noble feelings. A mere four months later, as I watched families shopping for Christmas, the emphasis was all too soon back on coveting the best toys, not sacrificially spending for the poor and needy and the children who were victims! It takes the Spirit of God to do a lasting work in our greedy selfish hearts. A servant spirit instead of a self-serving spirit is developed when we learn to give and not grab. If we could only start to recognize a covetous attitude as soon as it raises its ugly head, then deal with it in the power of the Spirit, we would bring blessing to ourselves and others.

Wanting a Better Position
It is just as much a sin to covet a position as it is to covet a posses-sion. When we first started the women's Bible study in our church, a godly woman was chosen to teach it. Soon I became aware of grum-bling and grousing going on in the ranks. Another woman felt that she should be teaching. She coveted the position given to the leader and began to undermine her ministry. She allowed herself to envy the woman who had been selected and decided if she could not do the teaching, then no one should. She succeeded in disrupting things to such an extent that we had to stop for a while and begin again later.

You can be on the other end of this, too. It might not be you who is doing the envying. I was trying to get a women's ministry off the ground in the church and decided to organize a day for women. I chose a young woman to teach one of the three sessions with me. This woman then asked why I had given myself two sessions and had given her only one.

I was overcome! *How could I have done this?* I wondered. Was I thinking more of my gift than I should? Had I been proud and in-sensitive? I decided I should have done as she suggested. I was just about to apologize and give her the opportunity when a godly older woman who had been with me when I was rebuked called me on the phone.

"Jill," she began, "this is not right. Don't change anything. This is a case of envy. You are the gifted teacher. We asked you to do this for us. It was sweet of you to invite another woman to take a session, but she is jealous of you and is causing problems behind your back. Anyway," she finished, "God has put you on a candlestick in our church to illuminate our minds from the Scriptures, so now get back up there and shine!"

It was very difficult for me to do what she advised, but I listened to her. I eventually told the woman causing me problems that the program would stay as it was, since that was what the women in the church wanted. She was very upset, and I never did manage to reconcile with her. In fact, she left the church soon after the incident. Sometimes these situations don't work out. But remember, you are only responsible for your own attitude and not other people's. There is an art to letting go. In the incident I have just related, I needed to come to the point of letting go of my part before I could discern what to do about it.

Don't Be a Monkey

When I was traveling in a country where there were lots of monkeys, a trapper told me how they caught the animals. They used jars with narrow necks and put some enticing food inside. A monkey would come along and put its fist inside the jar to get the food; then it would try to draw its fist out again. Of course, now the fist was larger than when it was relaxed, and it would not come out of the jar. The monkey would be truly trapped because it would not let go. All it had to do was open its fist, but it would not! The moral of the story, of course, is "Don't be a monkey!" It is a silly monkey that hangs on to something that has trapped him when all he needs to do is let go. Yet all of us, if we are honest, can sometimes see ourselves as silly monkeys. Letting go of a prized desire is a hard thing to do, but it must be done if we are not to be trapped. If you catch yourself hanging on to a desire when you should let it go, think of the monkey! Get on your knees and open your hand. Get it out of the jar.

When Wanting More Gets out of Hand

Only the love of God can overcome our natural tendency toward envy. Let us look at a couple of Bible people who dealt with envy and discover the problem it caused.

In I Samuel 18:1-4 we read the story of David and his friend Jonathan. They loved God, and they loved each other. "There was an immediate bond of love between them, and they became the best of friends" (I Samuel 18:1). Their friendship sustained them in the dark and dreadful days in which they lived. David had come into

King Saul's employment when a court official reported David's talent in playing the harp. Saul was suffering from bouts of deep melancholy, so he brought the young David to court to play for him when these dark moods came on him.

All went well until David began to be popular. He killed Goliath and became something of a folk hero. The women of Israel fell in love with the handsome youth, and when David returned from killing the Philistines in a later battle, the women came out from all the towns of Israel to meet the army with singing and dancing. The Bible then tells us what happened. "This was their song: 'Saul has killed his thousands, and David his ten thousands!' This made Saul very angry. 'What's this?' he said. 'They credit David with ten thousands and me with only thousands. Next they'll be making him their king!' So from that time on Saul kept a jealous eye on David" (I Samuel 18:7-9). Things went from bad to worse. Saul was being eaten alive by jealousy. So bad did Saul's envy become that he tried to kill David! Saul envied David's popularity, his Spirit-filled life, his courage, his skill as a warrior, musician, and poet. He said in his heart, "I want what he's got." Then he allowed this spirit of envy to grow into deep bedrock jealousy, and in the end it led to attempted murder. "I don't want him to have it either," he was saying.

Perhaps you don't think envy could drive you that far—but never underestimate the power of envy. Many have done much evil simply because they wanted something so badly they couldn't let it go.

On the opposite end of the spectrum was Jonathan, King Saul's son who was in line for the throne. But Jonathan loved David. Love overcame any envy Jonathan might have felt. Jonathan decided that David could have the throne and he would serve him. That's what love can do.

Now let's move on later into David's life. To his credit, even though David wanted the throne of Israel (he had already been anointed king, so it was a "done deal"), he refused to do evil in order to get it. As Saul forced David to run for his life, David never turned on Saul.

Unfortunately, David's moral character wasn't as strong when it came to beautiful women.

Of course, we are tempted to believe that coveting is not as bad a sin as, say, murder or adultery. Yet as the Bible points out, coveting can lead to worse sins. When you read the account of David and Bathsheba in 2 Samuel 11, you can see how David broke many other commandments when he took Bathsheba home to his bed.

King David wanted something that didn't belong to him, namely Bathsheba. She was the wife of David's neighbor. Once David saw this beautiful woman, he began planning how to obtain the forbidden object. Bathsheba was married to Uriah, one of David's best fighting men. After David slept with Bathsheba and she became pregnant, David called Uriah back from the war. He told Uriah to go home to his wife. This way David hoped to cover up his sin. Everyone would think the baby was Uriah's if he had been home from the war. But Uriah wouldn't go home. He stayed that night at the palace entrance with some servants. "Uriah replied, 'The Ark and the armies of Israel and Judah are living in tents, and Joab and his officers are camping in the open fields. How could I go home to wine and dine and sleep with my wife? I swear that I will never be guilty of acting like that'" (2 Samuel 11:11). The next night David got Uriah drunk just to make sure he went home, but Uriah again refused. Uriah turned out to be a better man drunk than David was sober!

So Uriah went back to the war without going home for the night, and in his hand was a letter from David to Joab, the commander of his forces. In the letter the king told Joab to station Uriah on the front lines and in the heat of the battle to withdraw from him, leaving him unprotected. Uriah carried and delivered his own death warrant to Joab. So this brave and loyal soldier died.

I wonder if David ever told Bathsheba what he had done. The Bible says that David thought he had gotten away with it, but "the Lord was very displeased with what David had done" (2 Samuel 11:27).

What disaster followed! This unrestrained desire led David to commit adultery and then murder. He killed Uriah as surely as if he himself had plunged the sword into his heart. Nathan the prophet, speaking for God, told the king, "I gave you [Saul's] house and his wives and the kingdoms of Israel and Judah. And if that had not been enough, I would have given you much, much more. Why, then, have you despised the word of the Lord and done this horrible deed? For you have murdered Uriah and stolen his wife" (2 Samuel 12:8-9).

David allowed coveting to grow into such jealousy he could not stand the thought of another man possessing the woman he wanted. Nathan pointed out that David had "despised the word of the Lord." Which word had David despised? The word that was written with the finger of God on tablets of stone! David began by breaking the first of the Ten Commandments, to love God alone. David allowed his desire for Bathsheba to become more important than obedience to God. He made her his idol, thereby breaking another commandment. He did not love his neighbor (Uriah the Hittite, Bathsheba's husband) as himself. He lied to Uriah, he stole his wife, he committed adultery, and he committed murder. David broke at least seven of the Ten Commandments when he coveted another man's wife. That's scary!

LOVE — THE CURE FOR COVETING

What about you? Does someone in your life cause you to be jealous and envious? How do you overcome this? How can you love others as much as you love yourself? How can you overcome a covetous spirit?

First, get on your knees and give up your rights. Maybe you have a right to have the thing the other person has. Be willing to give it up anyway. Then let God fill up your heart without it. God can make you as happy without the thing as with it.

Be constantly in prayer. Talk to God about the temptation you are having to covet someone or something. Don't try to fight it all by yourself. You are not strong enough. Prayer puts you in touch with the power of God. The basis of all prayer is helplessness. Cast yourself on him, and ask him to forgive your sin of coveting. Draw on his Spirit to fill your yearning heart. He will hear and answer.

Ask another person to battle through the temptation with you. Seek out a mature and safe person to support you in your struggle. Sometimes being able to share your situation releases you from the inner turmoil and sets you free.

Be Trusting

I remember talking to a friend about a struggle I had when I was a young Christian. I was struggling with the desire to get married. I had prayed long and earnestly for a partner, but no partner had materialized. Finally I confided this to a friend. She listened carefully and prayerfully and then suggested I make a list of all the things that my "ideal" man would be like. Then she said I should kneel down and talk to God about my list.

So I did what she suggested. "Lord," I said, "look at my list. But I am willing to do without a man," I added fervently, hoping he would be so impressed with my prayer that he would give me a husband immediately!

Instead, I distinctly heard him say, *Give me the list!*

I remember clenching my fist around that list, just like those monkeys had clenched their fists around the food in the jars. It took a long time to let go as I wrestled there on my knees. I wanted a husband so badly. I was fed up with going to my friends' weddings! With being the bridesmaid instead of the bride. I wanted what they had. I envied their happiness. So I knelt by my bedside and imagined two nail-pierced hands ready to receive that piece of paper with all of my hopes and dreams written on it. At last, I allowed it to fall onto the bed, into his hands. I cried a few tears. Then I made sure I stayed there until his transforming work was done in me. When it was over, I could say, "You know you have my heart's desire" and know he knew I meant it. "Keep my list safe, Lord, and do with it as you wish," I prayed.

He said, *Thank you,* and it was over! I know he smiled. It was so wonderful to open my hands and just let it go. From that time on I was truly free from eyeing every man I met with a view to being a suitable candidate for a husband. The freedom was palpable.

Be in the Word

And yet it is never over! As I lived free from that devouring necessity to be married, in his time God gave me a man that matched that list! *Surely now I will be free of a covetous spirit,* I thought. And yet a few years into our marriage I found myself struggling with envy all over again.

It happened when Stuart and I were serving a youth mission. Fortunately I knew I needed to be in the Word, and this helped me to recognize the warning signs. Whenever I began battling the spirit of covetousness, I read the Bible a lot, looking for verses that directly applied to my situation. I became jealous of all the time the other wives on the mission station had with their husbands. *Why does my husband have to be away all the time?* I asked myself. I was jealous of the nights my fellow missionary wives had together with their men! But I got in the Word, and I searched it for clues.

One day I read the parable of the laborers in the vineyard. The workers in the parable got in an argument about how much money their boss paid them. The boss answered, in no uncertain terms, "Don't I have the right to do what I want with my own money? Or are you envious because I am generous?" (Matthew 20:15, NIV).

I sat still after reading that and thought about it. Of course it was lawful for the owner of the vineyard to treat his workers as he saw fit! It was *his* vineyard and *his* money, and they were *his* workers. I knew God wanted me to apply this parable to my own situation. At last I was able to get on my knees and say, "I don't doubt it's lawful for you to do whatever you want with your own. Stuart is your own. So it is not up to me to tell you where he should work or when he will work or how long he will work. He is one of your laborers in your vineyard. I know it's lawful, but it feels awful! Anyway, God, do with Stuart what you will."

What a huge relief! I gave up the insistence of having my own way. Then God filled my heart with love for him and for my husband, and I stopped envying those who had their husbands at home.

The relief was the same as I had experienced that day long ago when I had first written my list and let it fall into God's hands.

So be in the Word. Apply it to your situation.

Be Obedient

You know coveting is wrong. It is sin, and you know what you need to do with that. Repent. Love for the Lord promotes obedience. "If you love me, obey my commandments," Jesus said (John 14:15). And what does he command? "A new command I give you: Love one another. As I have loved you, so you must love one another" (John 13:34, NIV). His commandment is to love one another. So we just need to obey him.

Well, how do we do that? Such love is without envy—for love "does not envy" (1 Corinthians 13:4, NIV). Anyone can be obedient—just do as you're told! When you love this way, all your relationships will benefit and so will you! The "green monster" of jealousy will no longer gobble you up. You will be free! Imagine a life free from wanting! A life of sweet contentment whether married or single, sick or healthy, rich or poor, beautiful or plain. Imagine a life of rest from striving and trying to manipulate things or wrest things from people. Imagine a tranquility of order in your soul. It can happen. It is up to you!

THE SECRET OF CONTENTMENT IS CHRIST

Paul wrote that he had learned the secret of contentment, and the secret was Christ. "I have learned to be content whatever the circumstances. I know what it is to be in need, and I know what it is to have plenty. I have learned the secret of being content in any and every situation, whether well fed or hungry, whether living in plenty or in want. I can do everything through him who gives me strength" (Philippians 4:11-13, NIV). Or in *The Message:*

> Actually, I don't have a sense of needing anything personally. I've learned by now to be quite content whatever my circumstances. I'm just as happy with little as with much,

with much as with little. I've found the recipe for being happy whether full or hungry, hands full or hands empty. Whatever I have, wherever I am, I can make it through anything in the One who makes me who I am.

I came to understand that contentment is a learned art. I can go to the "school of hard knocks" like Paul did and there learn how to be content with Christ alone. God would certainly give me plenty of chances to be in situations in which I could learn that the love of Jesus could fill my "if onlys" if only I would let him. I could be content wherever I was, whatever I had, or with whoever was with me in life. It was a choice I had to make—a choice to allow the Spirit to grow me up in Christ, out of my childishness, into maturity.

Paul says that love and contentment go together. That's why love does not covet. If left to itself, coveting grows horns and wings. It develops overnight into a big monster, and then you can be in big trouble.

Do you struggle with the monsters of jealousy and discontent? Do you feel you have never really found true satisfaction in this life whatever your circumstances, even though you are a Christian? Have you ever asked yourself, *Is this all there is?* And are you concerned about it? Good! Then we can hope that you will pursue the fine art of contentment. It can be learned by eager pupils. Paul said so.

He said he had *learned* how to be content whether full or empty, happy or sad, abased or abounding. He wrote his epistle of joy from prison! We might be in the prison of a bad marriage, of a chronic illness, of a heartbreaking circumstance. We may feel we are shut up to old age, poverty, or ignorance. Whatever prison God has allowed in our lives, his love can flood that cell and bring peace, contentment, and even joy. Paul showed us he was content with the love of Christ, and that love brought him contentment every day of his life. Paul was sick in body but healthy in soul. He was free from the deadly disease of coveting. He didn't even envy those outside his prison walls!

If the content of my contentment is Christ, then it follows that my relationship with him must be healthy and growing. What does it mean to be satisfied with Jesus? We hear a lot of talk about this, but what are the elements that make it work? Sit back for a moment and ask yourself some serious questions:

- Do you love being alone, or can't you be by yourself for very long?
- Do you always have to have people around you?
- Do you have a huge need to always be at meetings or to be out and about?
- What do you do with solitude? Do you fill it with noise? Is silence threatening to you?
- Do you grow impatient when you are reading the Bible? Do you keep your eye on the clock all the time?

Evidence of Contentment with Christ
You will know that you are learning contentment in your relationship with Christ when:

1. *You don't want to get up off your knees when you pray.* Do you seek out times of stillness and silence? In Exodus 33 Moses pitched a tent outside the camp. God's glory came down in the form of a cloud. This cloud was the visible and tangible evidence of the invisible God. The Bible says that in this Tent of Meeting the Lord met with Moses "face to face, as a man speaks to his friend" (Exodus 33:11). The verse goes on to say that after Moses left the tent, Joshua, his young assistant, "stayed behind in the Tent of Meeting." I am sure he could not drag himself away. There should be something of this experience for us when we meet with God. The Tent of Meeting is our own body, for our bodies are the "temple of the Holy Spirit" (I Corinthians 6:19). Now we can meet with him all day, every day, for he indwells us and has promised never to leave us or forsake us.

Think of the experience you have had of meeting with a wonderful friend. Your best friend. You think of ways to prolong your time together, don't you? You aren't looking at the clock, anxiously waiting for your time together to end. If you can begin to have times like this with God and he becomes your friend, you will not find yourself envying the friendships others have.

2. You make a decision not to grieve him. The Bible says we are not to grieve the Holy Spirit who lives in us (Ephesians 4:30). Our friendship with God will depend on our doing our part to keep short accounts with him. As soon as you know you have done something to hurt him, take time to make up.

Not long ago a close friend did something that hurt me. She realized at once what she had done to upset me, and she immediately got on the phone and apologized. I forgave her freely. We work together, and about four weeks later I noticed that she had not been staying around to chat over lunch as she usually did. One day she stopped me in the corridor and asked a little anxiously, "Are we all right, Jill?"

I knew what she meant. She wanted to know if the thing had been settled, if there was anything else that needed to be done to clear the path and restore our friendship.

"Yes, we're all right," I answered.

"Good," she replied with a grin. "I just wanted to make sure."

We should want to make sure, too. Our relationship with God should be so important to us that we want to make sure everything is all right. We may have confessed our sin, but if there is anything left to be said or done, we must attend to it in order that fellowship can be fully restored. Once our friendship is hurt, all steps need to be taken in order that we don't start to make substitutes for this most important friendship.

When we truly sense that we're "all right" with God, we will discover that we don't need to envy because we don't need anything else at all!

3. You focus on the best things in life that are free. Like your salvation, for example, or God's gifts of nature. We forget about these when our minds are focused on what we don't have, what we want, what we covet. If we focused on his free gifts of salvation, life, health, nature, and love, we would not be coveting plastic beauty and substitute pleasures. Besides, those things cost money we don't have and time we should be giving to others. Try counting your blessings. When you focus on what's best, you won't be coveting anything else!

One day not long ago a little girl wrote a love poem on her stepmom's computer. The mom had been worrying about buying her daughter clothes so she could have what other little girls her age had. The poem was unbelievable. It was all about the things the little girl wished for her stepmom. Each line began with, "I wish for you . . ." She ended the poem with "Because I love you!"

The stepmom told me about the poem. We cried together. "You can't buy this," I said. "There's not enough money in the world!" She agreed. It was priceless. As we work for these things in our lives, we will find ourselves not bothering too much with material worries. And we will be grateful and satisfied with love.

MAKING IT MINE

These questions can be used for personal quiet time or adapted for group discussions. A notebook, a Bible, and a pencil would be useful.

Thinking It Over

1. Read the Ten Commandments in Exodus 20. Why is coveting so dangerous?
2. Define coveting in your own words.
3. Give an example of little children envying each other. How does this reflect behavior in the church?
4. Think about the story of David and Jonathan in 1 Samuel 18. How did their strong love for each other overcome envy?
5. Share a situation in which you had to let go of something you wanted very badly. How did God help you to do that?
6. Think about the monkeys holding on to the food in the jar. What does this picture remind you of?

Praying It In

1. Reread the Ten Commandments. Think your way through all of them saying, "I'm sorry, Lord," where appropriate.
2. Focus on the list in the "covet" commandment. Ask yourself if you are coveting anything on this list. Talk to God about it.
3. If there is any list you need to make (like the one I made, a list of things you desire), make it and then give it to God.
4. Pray for your church. Is there envy and strife going on over positions, gifts, or leadership issues? Pray about this. Pray that love will prevail.
5. Pray for the same things for missionaries you support.
6. Pray for Christian leaders who are in the limelight. Pray that they will stay humble and usable.

Prayer

Release my grasp, Lord. Help me to let go of things I covet. Things I believe I must have to make me happy. Things I want to own. Some of these things are even out of bounds. Forgive me, Lord. Take my fingers, clutching on to my dreams, and help me to open my hands wide. Help me to trust you to take my dreams and longings and keep them for me. I know you love me. I can trust you. I will trust you—now.

And help me to major on my relationship with you, developing my prayer life, and keeping short accounts with you. Remind me that love relationships cannot be bought, for the best things in life are free. Help me to thank you for the love relationships in my life. Amen.

Living It Out

1. How will your behavior change because of the decisions you have made through this chapter on coveting?
2. How will your plans change?
3. Write a promise to God about this—then keep it!
4. Is there a person you should talk to about some of these issues? Who is that person? Make a plan for when and how you will do this. Follow through.
5. If you struggle with material wants, start to get rid of things you have in your house. Give them to someone in need.
6. If you are in a situation where you are tempted by another person, take steps to remove yourself—whether that person is a boss, a coworker, or someone at a health club. Don't walk straight into temptation and expect the Lord to deliver you from evil!

CHAPTER SIX

LOVING WHEN WE'RE PROVOKED

An angry man stirs up dissension.
PROVERBS 29:22 (NIV)

LOVE "IS NOT EASILY ANGERED," SAYS I CORINTHIANS 13:5 (NIV). In other words, love isn't touchy, it doesn't fly off the handle, it isn't a warmonger. "Then why are so many Christians losing it? Why are there so many church fights?" you may ask.

Good questions.

I was talking to a disillusioned churchgoer who had just left his church because one more knock-down-drag-out fight was brewing and he had no stomach for it. "If Christians are full of the love of God like they say they are, then why are church people so touchy?" he asked me. "How is it there are so many disagreeable people in church? Why can't they handle their differences with grace and charity? Why are too many churches like war zones?"

"True love isn't quick to take offense," I answered. "There's a breakdown in the church between what we believe and how we behave. When we practice loving others like we should, we become peacemakers, not warmongers."

"Well," said the man, "I have enough conflict at work. I don't need it when I go to church. If I could find a bunch of people loving each other like they should, I'd join! Till then, I'll worship God on the golf course!"

SPOILING FOR A FIGHT

There is no question that it's much easier to start a fight than end one. Peace doesn't just happen all on its own either; someone has to make it happen. That's why the word *peace*maker gives us pause. It's much less work and so much more fun "stirring the pot" than getting the food on the table. There is something in all of us that is spoiling for a fight. It is called the "flesh," our "old nature." The flesh is always looking for a fight. Something in us wants to declare war on someone somewhere. The counteracting force in believers, however, is the Holy Spirit, who wants to call a truce and bring peace into the situation.

I can know if I am walking in the Spirit if I engage in peacemaking. Conversely, I can know if I am walking in the flesh if I am a warmonger. There are far too many warmongers around and not nearly enough peacemakers—especially in the church. Take the choir for instance. I remember someone quipping, "When the devil fell out of heaven, he fell into the choir!"

"Or the kitchen," someone else chuckled.

I suppose someone could have added, "Or the boardroom, staff room, drama department, or parking lot!" I remember first coming to our church in America and being appalled at the way people yelled at each other in the parking lot. I got up one Sunday and pled, "Please, can we have a whole lot more loving in the parking lot." Then there is the family. There is so much conflict between husbands and wives and between parents and children—and that includes Christian families.

Paul taught us that love isn't always spoiling for a fight; rather, it is always looking for a way to be constructive. So why are there so many difficult people in church? Because there isn't enough love going around!

BEING A PEACEMAKER

The idea of the phrase "Love is not easily angered" describes someone exercising restraint even when thoroughly provoked. In fact, a valid translation would be "Love isn't easily provoked." The church of Jesus Christ has a lot of people around who are very easily provoked. They are supersensitive, almost paranoid. They think there is someone lurking in the next pew or behind the coatracks who is out to get them! And on the other side of the coin, there is also a fair amount of provoking going on. But love doesn't lose it, and love doesn't cause it. What is more, love works actively to bring warring factions together and be the reconciler.

Paul wrote to the church in Philippi because he was concerned about a church fight he had heard about. Two prominent women named Euodia and Syntyche (my husband calls them "Odious" and "Soon Touchy") had gotten at odds with each other, and as usually happens, people were taking sides. A church split was in the cards (Philippians 4:2). Paul was concerned for his friends, wanting everyone to work for reconciliation. So he appealed to a "loyal yokefellow" (NIV) to help these two women to settle their disagreement. These women had worked side by side with Paul; in fact, they had "contended" (strong word) in the cause of the gospel together (Philippians 4:3). Apparently, they were leaders in the church and good friends of the apostle, but they had fallen out with each other. Paul wanted them to "fall in" with each other again.

It struck me as a tall order for this hapless male, whoever he was, to be instructed by the great apostle to get himself in between these two warring women and sort it all out. This was not an easy job! My husband quipped that this "loyal *yoke*fellow" was likely to get himself scrambled.

Anyway, he was to try to make peace happen. He was to play the role of a peacemaker. We have no record of whether he managed to do this or not. We don't even know if he tried. Perhaps we don't need to know. All we need to know is that Paul expected an ordinary, run-of-the-mill guy to try to help two ordinary, run-of-the-mill church ladies who were at odds to reconcile.

Sometimes it isn't two women who can't see eye-to-eye about things; sometimes it's a battle of the sexes, or even the generations. When we first came to pastor our church in Wisconsin, the year was 1970, and the hippie movement was in full swing. Kids were wearing the flag on their blue jeans, growing their hair long, and marching for peace. All they were doing in Milwaukee was engendering a war! Then came the Jesus movement, when lots of these same kids were reached for Christ and came tentatively into the church. We had a large influx of these young people through the ministry of a couple in our congregation.

Stuart and I had been working with a similar group of young people in Europe before emigrating to the States in 1970, so we were delighted to see these kinds of kids flocking to our church (incidentally, one of them is now our senior pastor!). Other members of our congregation were not so thrilled, however. The generation gap widened.

One night my husband had a visit from one of his leaders. "I want you to keep our church kids separate from these Jesus freaks," he said. We had a problem on our hands. My husband suggested that we start a Sunday school class called Generation Bridge. We would invite twelve people from the two disparate groups to participate in it, give them the book of James to study together, and see what transpired.

Each week we paired an "oldie" and a "youngie" together, a hippie and a nonhippie, a Jesus freak and a nonfreak. Then we had each pair study and present one of the lessons together. At the end of the six weeks, they didn't want to quit; in fact, there was a long line waiting to get into the class! We expanded the program and saw God move in our church in unprecedented ways.

The man who came to complain became the deacon overseeing the program, and God did the rest, bringing two very different groups of people together in Christ. This man became a true "yokefellow"! He was willing to allow his love for Christ to flow through him to some young people he had heartily disliked. Moreover, he was willing to be the vehicle for God's reconciling work. As he worked with the kids, the love of God took over and a miracle happened.

Some of us have a rare gift in this regard, and some of us don't have any gifts at all, much less the stomach for such a ministry. Those of us who hate confrontation, like me, run a mile when asked by some apostle Paul to insert ourselves into such a challenging mess. "I'm glad I'm not gifted for this," we mutter as we hurry by on the way to our church peer group. Yet the Holy Spirit is the great

Peacemaker, and we have all that we need to help bring about a happy end to an unhappy situation. It may be very difficult to offer to mediate in a church row, but many a hard thing can be accomplished with faith and love in the power of the Spirit. It could also be a matter of duty. *Duty* is an old-fashioned word that means "doing the right thing about a wrong thing, even when you would rather be doing another thing."

Maybe you are reading this and have an uneasy feeling that God is nudging you to be a peacemaker in a certain difficult situation. Why not stop right now and ask him for the love that you will need to obey? Love is a peacemaker, and God can fill you with all the love you need to initiate a truce or give you the grace to offer to mediate in a dispute that threatens the unity of the body. Tell the Lord you are willing to be a loyal yokefellow.

God doesn't want us saying, "I'm glad I'm not gifted in this area." He is looking for folks who are willing to be lovers of God and lovers of people and lovers of the body of Christ, whether they are gifted at it or not. He is looking for them to be loyal to him and obedient to his call.

PICKING OUR BATTLES

If conflict is not happening in the church, it is happening in the family. There are so many family members spoiling for a fight. Even Christians struggle within their own marriages or families. I had a huge response to a sermon that I preached not long ago called, "Christmas is coming and so are the relatives!"

When our daughter was thirteen, I went through the same thing mothers of teenagers go through all over the world. One night Judy went to bed a perfectly sweet child wanting nothing more than to please her parents above all things; she got up in the morning a complete stranger! At breakfast time she came around the corner of the kitchen spoiling for a fight. "Where's Mother?" her angry little face asked. Then as her eyes lighted on me, her body language was saying without doubt, "Come on then, let's have a fight!"

Who is this young woman? I wondered. Where had she come from, and how had she gotten into our home? How long would she be staying, and when would our sweet compliant daughter return? Then began that awful period called adolescence when mothers' and daughters' hormones are all at odds at the same time. It doesn't seem fair, does it? Judy and I couldn't see eye-to-eye on anything, or so it seemed. We struggled about clothes, movies, friends, makeup, homework, money, and anything else that was on the agenda for the day.

One day our daughter came into the living room just before church time. She was dressed in blue jeans. "Judy," I said briskly, "hurry up and get changed. We are late for church."

"I'm going like this," she announced defiantly and headed for the door.

I followed her down the hall, and we began to argue. My husband appeared and listened for a few moments. Then he said, "Do you two remember Muhammad Ali?" Well, we both stopped shouting at each other and looked at him, trying to figure out what on earth Muhammad Ali had to do with Judy's blue jeans!

"Ali had a trainer," Stuart continued, ignoring the atmosphere. "He allowed his trainer to pick his fights. As long as Ali let him choose whom he fought, he won. But one day he got a bit big for his boots (or his gloves). 'I'll pick whom I'll fight from now on,' he told his trainer. And against all protests he began to do so. One day he said to his manager, 'Get me the champ.'

"'You're not ready for the champ,' his manager objected. Ali insisted, and so very reluctantly the man agreed to fix it up. It was the beginning of the end for Ali. His trainer and manager had been right. He was not ready to fight the champ, and he went down hard, losing the bout."

My husband paused and then said to Judy and me, "If you two fight over every little thing that comes up, you'll have no strength left when the really big things happen that are worth fighting for—like moral issues, matters of life and death. There will be nothing left of your relationship if you sweat the small stuff."

He was right, and we knew it! From then on I tried to let God—my heavenly Trainer and Manager—pick my fights for me, and I know Judy tried to do the same. As each altercation came along, I said to the Lord, "Is this worth a fight or can I let it go?" If I sensed that it was really important—a biblical principle or a moral issue— I tried to fight fair. If it wasn't a "hill to die on," I tried to bite my tongue and let it go! Because I loved my little girl so much, I allowed love to decide what was really important and what was not. The night after the jeans war, Stuart said to me, "Jill, is a bit of cloth worth fighting about? Let's just be glad she still wants to go to church at all! We could be fighting a much bigger battle."

Love doesn't instigate a fight. Love seeks hard to find a compromise. It works hard at making peace, for peace doesn't just happen, it has to be *made!*

Are kids easily angered? Of course they are! Tempers flare readily all day long. Do they say, "Let's have a fight"? Of course they do! Sometimes the child has a right to be angry at a parent, and sometimes a parent has a right to be angry at a child. But there is a right kind of anger, and there is a wrong kind of anger.

FEELING RIGHTEOUS ANGER

First of all, we need to realize that some anger is legitimate. The Bible talks about "holy wrath" or "righteous anger." We have to be honest with ourselves here and call things by their real names. It's no good for us to tell a friend, "I was righteously angry with my husband today," if, quite frankly, we simply lost our temper! On the other hand, there are some things that are outrageously unfair, unkind, or downright evil, and there is something wrong with us if we don't get mad about them. Righteous anger is love in tears.

Love in Tears

Love in tears that refuses to be consoled is love that determines to make a difference in a bad situation. Love doesn't know what it means to be dry-eyed in the face of the appalling need we bump into day by daily day. Love in tears wipes the faces of little children abused by rough adults. Love in tears doesn't sleep well at night when faced with someone else's pain.

I remember experiencing this righteous anger when Stuart and I were in Russia. One day the missionary we were with took us to visit the Kremlin. A couple of teenage girls stood by the guard at the gate to have their picture taken, rather like the way tourists do in London at Buckingham Palace. They had had to step over a low chain separating the guards from the tourists. At once, three or four police descended on the kids, took hold of their arms, and pushed them off the grass. One of the girls gave the policeman a cheeky retort. Then they were taken off to a little hut by the side of the road.

The missionary we were with was worried. "Men here have a bad attitude toward women," she explained. "They will treat those girls harshly."

Six hours later we passed that way again. The girls were still at the hut. Now they were all in tears. One was on the ground sobbing. The men stood around shouting and harassing them. They would not let the girls go home. Our friend walked up to the group of police and went to bat for the young teenagers. We could not understand what she was saying, but she argued forcefully and with spirit and succeeded in getting girls free. She was in tears on her return to us. She was also very angry. "We see so much of this bullying of women in this society," she said. "It is in part a holdover from the cold war. I get so angry!"

I admired her spunk, but then love is spunky when it sees injustice and always goes to bat for the underdog. That's how love behaves!

I will never forget traveling to Cambodia to make a film for World Relief. We were to actually make the documentary in the "killing fields," part of which are now a museum. In the center of the open graveyard there is a glass monument with hundreds of skulls in it. The filming was more than hard! I found myself getting more and more angry as I met victims who had lost their entire families to the murderous Khmer Rouge, the ruthless ruling government of that dark time just a few years ago.

This righteous anger drives one to try to change things, to say, "If there is anything I can do to stop this sort of atrocity from ever happening again, I will do it!"

The righteous anger that Stuart and I felt about this war that killed so many innocent people led us to go back to our church, share the need, and start a ministry. We began supporting the churches in Cambodia and helping them to establish health clinics, community banking, and spiritual instruction. Today, as a result, literally thousands of Cambodian children are in groups learning, as one little child put it, about "germs and Jesus." One hundred and sixteen churches have been planted in that once-horrible place, and it all started when we got angry enough to do something about it!

Love allows us to be this sort of angry. Love helps us to turn our thoughts and hearts toward others and their needs and away from our own. This sort of anger, righteous anger, can lead to constructive action. We can find power to change a bit of the situation that causes the anger.

DEALING WITH UNRIGHTEOUS ANGER

But then there is the other sort of anger, the wrong sort, called unrighteous anger. The sort we have to handle rightly or it will handle us. Wrong anger pushes us to attack.

Altercations usually begin with being irritable. Irritability is the launching pad for anger. It makes us vulnerable to anger and robs us of our joy. We find ourselves grinding our teeth if we are sixth in the line at the checkout counter. Now with the restrictions at the airports, it's easy to lash out at the people scanning our luggage or picking us out for one more body check. We find ourselves growing increasingly hostile toward the people who are only trying to keep us safe.

Hostility is anger that has turned aggressive. We see the person we are angry with as the enemy. We don't want to make peace; we just want to keep the argument going. This can even lead to violence.

So how on earth can an angermonger be changed into a peacemaker? The more we allow the love of God to be shed abroad in our hearts by the Holy Spirit, the more we will experience love holding back our temper like a bridle holds back a horse, preventing us from descending into ferocity. We live in a ferocious world, but love is gentle and kind, patient in the face of such behavior, responding quietly and peaceably to provocation.

I have thought about that phrase, "We live in a ferocious world," many times since September 11. Surely that is true! There is so much carnage in the world, so much hate, so many seething angers. Generations of animosity are breaking out everywhere. And those who are the peacemakers seem to be so very few and far between! I have begun to understand how difficult it is to *make* peace happen. But just because it is difficult doesn't mean we shouldn't try. And just because it may not work out doesn't mean we should not stick our necks out, for this is what we are called to do. Jesus said being peacemakers would single us out from the pack. Not only that, he promised we would find happiness in the work. "Blessed are the peacemakers," he told his disciples. "Blessed" because "they will be called sons of God" (Matthew 5:9, NIV). So whether we are hard at work making peace at home, in the workplace, in school, in our marriage and family, or even in the wider world, we can know the smile of God on our efforts to make peace.

But this peace we must try to make is not "peace at any price." That is often capitulation. Peace can sometimes be won only through a battle. Sometimes you have to fight a tyrant like the world fought Hitler in the Second World War. But often consultation, negotiation, and a whole lot of wise words can avoid a battle! Most of all, other people's anger can be overcome by prayer and love— sheer agape love.

If you are on your way out the door to try to mediate a dispute, don't go before you have soaked the whole thing in prayer. It does no good to try valiantly, fail miserably, and then come home and pray furiously! Instead, first pray furiously, after that, try valiantly, and then if you fail miserably, you will hear the Lord say, "Thank you for trying. Well done, good and faithful servant." You will even find yourself willing to try valiantly again, just for the incredible joy of hearing his, "Well done!"

Make Your Own Peace First

Prayer and peace go together, which brings me to the next thing. If you are going to be a peacemaker between angry people, you will need to be spiritually healthy yourself. That's where lots of prayer comes in! If you have not dealt with your own issues of anger through prayer, confession, and restitution, you cannot very well help others to deal with their problems. You can suppress your anger and cause yourself ill health, or you can confess your anger and put it where it belongs—at the foot of the cross. Once you have dealt with your own anger, whether it be righteous anger or unrighteous anger, you will be in a position to help others deal with theirs.

If you would like some words to help you confess some suppressed anger, you could stop here and borrow my words, or, of course, you can use your own. Let prayer bring you to a place of personal peace and usefulness:

> *Lord, I have been so angry for so long I can't remember what it feels like to be free of this deep agitation inside me. Nothing seems to touch it. Nothing seems to mend it. Only you can get down there and release me from this destructive force of anger that wells up inside me all too often. I could almost say I fear for my actions when this obsessive anger takes over my soul. Forgive me for the bad anger and teach me self-control. Then help me to change what I can in the situation, Lord. Give me peace and make me a peacemaker. Thank you! Amen.*

Control the Tongue

One of the problems with anger that is out of control is that we say things we can never take back. Once those angry words are out of our mouths, they never return. The damage is done, and sometimes it is irreparable.

James, the brother of our Lord Jesus, painted several interesting word pictures when he talked about the trouble that our angry tongues can cause. "The tongue," says James, "is a small thing, but what enormous damage it can do. A tiny spark can set a great forest on fire." He describes the tongue as a fire with blazing power to destroy. He tells us, "It is set on fire by hell itself" (James 3:5-6).

Once such a fire is blazing, it is almost impossible to stop it. It is like a forest fire that is raging out of control.

Then James uses a couple more pictures. A huge boat can be turned at will by a tiny rudder; a horse can be led by a tiny bit. In the same way, our tongues need a bridle and a bit. If we are able to bridle our tongues, it will be because Jesus is "riding" our lives and controlling all our members in the same way that a person riding a horse controls it. Think about the Lord Jesus riding into Jerusalem on that young donkey. We may picture a docile little donkey picking its way placidly through surging crowds who are shouting and waving leafy branches in its face. But we must remember that the little donkey was unbroken until someone brought it to Jesus and he sat on it! Once the Lord was on its back, it became controlled by another Spirit altogether. It was broken in.

We need to be "broken in," too! Jesus must take us in hand. All our wild-donkey nature and our stubborn ways need to be put in the control of his nail-pierced hands. Then with the reins of our lives in his control, people can be as irritating as they like. We will keep our little hooves moving forward, whatever leafy things are in our faces and whoever is trying to trip us up. If Jesus is in control, he will guide and lead us.

Have we allowed Jesus to put a bit and bridle on us? Self-control is God-control!

Self-control is a fruit of the Spirit (Galatians 5:22-23). Being a peacemaker means that God will need to control your tongue, so you will need to be full of the Spirit. "A gentle answer turns away wrath" (Proverbs 15:1); "A fool gives full vent to anger, but a wise person quietly holds it back" (Proverbs 29:11). As I make sure Christ is controlling my life and the Spirit is growing his patience and self-control in me, I will become a blessing in conflicts in the family and in the church.

Don't Keep Accounts
Paul tells us that love "keeps no record of wrongs" (I Corinthians 13:5, NIV). Love doesn't pick fights, but it also doesn't keep a running record of someone else's wrongs.

When someone has hurt us, perhaps verbally, and those cruel words have been said and have lodged in our thinking, it is hard not to keep a running record on the one who caused us so much pain. Now here is a chance to really see ourselves as others see us. Do kids remember the evil said or done to them on the school playground— or worse, said by a parent who tells them they are no good and they never should have been born? Yes. Do adults remember hurtful words? Yes! But Paul said we need to mature past this. As we grow up in Christ, we should be able to learn the art of forgiving those who hurt and harm us, not keeping them accountable forever. This is certainly easier preached than practiced. It is awfully hard not to harbor a grudge, yet love lets go of the wrongs done to it. Forgiveness relinquishes the right to vengeance. Vengeance belongs to God, and he will repay. Justice needs to be done, and we can expect people to be accountable for crimes and wrongs done, but vengeance is not our business.

The Bible says, "If your brother sins, rebuke him, and if he repents, forgive him" (Luke 17:3, NIV). But what if he doesn't repent? Then I hold myself ready to say, "I forgive you" if the time ever comes; but in the meantime, I refuse to harbor anger, bitterness, or resentment.

I was teaching in a Bible college not too long ago, and a young girl was assigned to look after me. She was beautiful, godly, and bright. She was a chartered accountant and was putting herself through college while keeping her career going. At the end of my week, I was eating dinner with her and teased her about not being married. "How did you escape?" I kidded her.

She didn't reply for a moment; then she said hesitantly, "I was married."

"I'm so sorry," I said. "I didn't know."

"That's all right," she said. And I could see that it was. It wasn't all right that her husband had walked out on her in a particularly cruel way, but it was "all right" in her heart. It was well with her soul. Peace like a river flowed there. She had been able to let go of the terrible wrong done to her. What was more, the Lord had helped her to look at the future as God's future for her, and she insisted on seeing a better day ahead. True love from God keeps you from being discouraged.

"But you don't know how my spouse treated me," an abandoned man once told me. "Let me tell you . . . ," he began.

But I stopped him. I knew it would not help him to tell the sad story one more time. I have observed what someone has said: "Some people destroy their relationship by writing everything down with the 'pencil of memory' but never take anything off with the 'eraser of forgiveness.'" In contrast, my young friend had been busy with her eraser!

This young woman at Bible college shared very few of the salient points of her story with me. She gave me the bare bones and spared me, and herself, the details. I knew she had left a multitude of information out of her brief account, but she refused to wallow in self-pity, and she had not kept an account of every sin. She had forgiven him. Not that he had sought her forgiveness, but she stood ready to say, if he ever did get around to asking her, "I forgive you fully and freely as Christ has forgiven me!"

What's Hanging around Your Mind?

Years ago my husband was on a missionary trip to a primitive tribe. When he and the missionary he was traveling with arrived late in an isolated village, there was nowhere to stay for the night but the witch doctor's house. It was not surprising that they had a fitful night! All the ominous paraphernalia hanging from the high grass roof fascinated Stuart.

"What are all those objects hanging down?" he asked the missionary.

"That's his bookkeeping system," he replied. "Whenever someone in the village offends him or hurts one of his kids, he hangs an object of some sort up there to remind him of the wrong done to his family. It would be a terrible thing if he ever let himself forget what they did."

"How primitive," I hear you saying. "No wonder we need to

send missionaries to these primitive tribes." But wait a bit! How much garbage have you and I got hanging around the roofs of our minds? Do we go to sleep determined to remember everything and wake up determined never to forget anything? Love doesn't keep a running record of someone else's wrongdoings. It's funny, no one ever forgets where they bury the hatchet.

Love is slow to anger and quick to forgive. My friend set out to forget the details of her husband's rejection and abandonment. She was equipping herself for ministry, and I knew the Lord loved her for it. She was truly a girl after God's own heart!

So how can I bear the grief and pain of rejection or betrayal without it destroying me? And if I have been so badly rejected, how can I ever love again? Well, that is what the love of God does so well in us and through us. In a spectacular way, love bears all things. Love loves again and again and again! That's how love behaves.

But it will take some time, so give yourself time. If you have been hurt, you need to

- spend time healing. Don't rush into another relationship too soon. Give yourself a chance to get well.
- spend time "minding your mind." Concentrate on the things that have been good—good memories, for example. Paul said, "Fix your thoughts on what is true and honorable and right. Think about things that are pure and lovely and admirable. Think about things that are excellent and worthy of praise" (Philippians 4:8). You mind your mind, and God will mind your heart!
- spend time revisiting your theology. Remind yourself of the promises of God. God loves you. God forgives you. God provides for you. God has plans for you. God is with you. God will give you help. God will empower you.
- spend time being quiet. Love grows in quiet places. Wait on the Lord. Refocus your attention on your personal relationship with him rather than your personal relationship with others.
- spend time reading the Word of God, not just snatching a

few verses of Scripture as you dash out the door into the rest of your life. Bask in it. Soak in it. Drink it in. Read, mark, and inwardly digest it. Let the Word of God comfort you as only the Word of God can. Just give yourself time.

BURYING THE PAST

After giving yourself time, you will find love growing inside you, and with the growth of love, forgiveness. You will find yourself discovering the ability to cope. Love "bears all things," Paul says (I Corinthians 13:7, NKJV). And what is more, it always protects the ones it loves. Love doesn't always seek to expose the bad stuff. It covers over the ugly in someone's life. That's why love doesn't gossip. Gossip sees to it that someone's faults are kept in the news; love refuses to do that. Proverbs 10:12 says, "Hatred stirs up quarrels, but love covers all offenses." In fact, love refuses to drag the skeleton out of the closet. It buries the past and refuses to rob the tomb.

That means that love must then bear a lot. The word picture of love bearing all things can be used in a variety of ways. First, it can be used for the roof of a building. A roof keeps the things inside it out of sight. Love keeps the lid on bits of juicy information.

Second, the word can be used to describe something that is watertight, like a ship. Are you watertight? Can you listen to fascinating details of a story and be watertight? Or do you leak?

Third, the word can be used to depict a high tower that is impervious to all attacks. Can you be impervious to all assaults on the knowledge you have locked up inside you? Those of us who listen to the problems of others must keep our counsel and the respect of the one who has trusted us with potentially damaging information.

Fourth, the word can be used to describe pillars that bear a heavy weight. Sometimes I am told things in confidence that are a heavy weight on my mind and heart. It would help so much to share the burden of the knowledge with someone else. But love has broad shoulders; it can bear an enormous load. It doesn't mean love's shoulders won't be bent with the weight of it all, but they will bear the load of confession well, because that's how love behaves. That is what love is, and that is what love does!

Finally, the word *bears* can also be used for a mantle or cloak—a huge warm mantle to cover, conceal, and warm the wearer. Love is like a huge heavenly blanket that runs around our weary, hurting world throwing itself over the one who needs to be loved, whatever he or she has done. Yes, there is a covering quality to love!

Unfortunately, some people are so leaky that they can't wait to pass on scandal or hearsay about people. And sometimes they use, of all things, the prayer meeting! It is easier to pass on information they should be keeping to themselves with their eyes shut rather than open! This is totally out of order, but I have heard it done: "Oh, Lord, please help Joan Smith to resist temptation at work," or "Please help John to know there is no sin too big to forgive." That sort of nonsense will put people on high alert and most likely increase the attendance at the prayer meeting. But that is not how love behaves.

Love gets angry at the right things, allows God to control its tongue, refuses to enjoy or pass on confidential information, and can, in fact, be trusted to keep its counsel and cover over the ugly in people's lives wherever possible.

Above all, love is not touchy, flying off the handle at the slightest thing. Love lives a peaceable life, being a reconciler and not a warmonger. How are you doing? How are you shaping up?

MAKING IT MINE

These questions can be used for personal quiet time or adapted for group discussions. A notebook, a Bible, and a pencil would be useful.

Thinking It Over

1. Are you prone to "losing it" easily? Have you found this has been better or worse since you became a Christian (be honest)? What sort of things send you over the edge?
2. Have you any experience with peacemaking in the family? in the workplace? in the world? Share.
3. Discuss the statement "Righteous anger is 'love in tears.'"
4. What is unrighteous anger? How do you know the difference?
5. Read James 3:2-6. Discuss it or write a summary of it in your own words.
6. Discuss the story of the missionary hut. What did you like about this illustration? What didn't you like?
7. Discuss the statement "Love buries the past and refuses to rob the tomb." Put this in your own words.
8. Have you ever been in a prayer meeting like the one described, where improper things were shared in prayer? How did it make you feel?
9. Share ways the Lord can help you to be slow to anger.
10. Which was the most convicting part of this chapter? the most encouraging part?

Praying It In

1. Pray for mothers of small children.
2. Pray for sick people.
3. Pray for caregivers of elderly parents.
4. Pray for people under stress at work.
5. Pray for people who are traveling.
6. Pray for relief and development agencies.

Living It Out

1. Tackle one area of your life at a time. Where will you start? When will you start? How will you start?
2. Write a note of apology to someone with whom you lost it recently. Mail it.

CHAPTER SEVEN

LOVING AND TRUSTING AGAIN

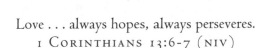

Love . . . always hopes, always perseveres.
1 CORINTHIANS 13:6-7 (NIV)

"HAS ANYONE EVER BETRAYED YOUR TRUST?" A YOUNG
woman asked me. Without waiting for a reply, she rushed on: "Do
you know how difficult it is to ever trust anyone again after that?"

It was hard to talk to her about hoping to love again. Yet true
love is able to love again, however badly it has been treated. God
himself is a perfect example. Love in the shape of Jesus was betrayed
and denied by his closest friends, yet he never stopped loving them,
and he trusted them again.

Love always trusts the loved one. There is a "covering quality" to
love. In fact, love is a harbor of trust for those who are doubted by
everyone else. Love finds the strength to trust twice, or three times,
or seventy times seven times!

This does not mean that love is blind; in fact, only love really
sees. Yet seeing what it sees and knowing what it knows, love makes
a decision to love and trust again.

LOVE LOOKS THROUGH THE DARKNESS TO THE DAWN

When Paul penned his portrait of love in 1 Corinthians 13, Jesus
sat for the portrait. When we follow Jesus through the Gospels, we
have plenty of pictures of what loving trust is all about. Love is always positive and affirming. It doesn't put people down, even when
things look pretty bad.

Jesus knew full well that his disciples would turn away from
him—for a time. Yet he didn't look at them and say to himself,

"I've got a bunch of losers here." Instead he said, "I've got a bunch of winners!" That was because he refused to stop believing in those men. Love "believes all things" (I Corinthians 13:7, NKJV).

Love looks through the present darkness and sees a new day dawning. Consider Peter, who was shooting off his mouth and saying, "I am ready to go to prison with you, and even to die with you." Jesus told him bluntly that Satan desired to have all of the disciples that he might sift them like wheat. But he added, "I have pleaded in prayer for you, Simon, that your faith should not fail" (Luke 22:31-33).

Here is a wonderful truth! Jesus was praying for Peter, and Jesus is praying for us. Hebrews tells us that Jesus "is able, once and forever, to save everyone who comes to God through him. He lives forever to plead with God on their behalf" (Hebrews 7:25). In the upper room just before the Lord went to the cross and then back to heaven, he prayed for all of us. What did he pray? He prayed that the Father would keep us from evil. "My prayer is not that you take them out of the world but that you protect them from the evil one" (John 17:15, NIV).

There is good news, and there is bad news about this prayer of Jesus. The good news is that Jesus is praying for us. The bad news is that he knows we will need it!

Jesus also prayed that we, his followers, would love each other, that we would enjoy unity. It really mattered to him that his children get along with each other. He prayed that we would "be united" (John 17:11). And he wanted us to love one another: "I have given them the glory you gave me, so that they may be one, as we are—I in them and you in me, all being perfected into one. Then the world will know that you sent me and will understand that you love them as much as you love me" (John 17:22-23).

This kind of love for one another will set us apart from the rest of the world. We believers are all very different people. However, when such different people can love one another so much, the world will take notice! That's why our love and our unity were so important to Jesus.

I can understand this. I remember sitting by my mother as she was dying. "I have something to ask you, Jill," she said to me. "I want you and Shirley [my sister] always to stay close." It had always been a deep desire of our mother that we stay in contact as we grew up, married, and went our separate ways.

"Yes, yes, Mother," I replied absently.

But I was to remember her wistful request many times as my own children grew up. It became incredibly important to me that my three grown children kept in touch and loved each other—to the point that it almost became an obsession! I had to give it to God and stop manipulating circumstances to make it happen.

Of course, you can't make it happen, but there is nothing wrong in wanting it to happen. I was delighted to read that love and unity among his children mattered to Jesus, too. So we can do what he did—pray about it and ask our kids to work at it. He did both of these things, and if he was praying about it then, you know he is praying about it for us now. He knows we need each other in this present evil age because that is what the family of God is for!

MEETING JESUS ON THE OTHER SIDE OF FAILURE

The disciples failed the test, of course. They squabbled and fell out with each other like all families do. But Jesus prayed for them and looked forward to the time when it would be different. He trusted them, and he entrusted them to God.

The devil tempts us in all sorts of ways, not least in our closest relationships. He hates us, and he wants us to hate each other. Jesus knows the devil is working hard to cause dissension. Satan wants to sift us like wheat. He wants to winnow us, and he will be permitted to winnow us. But like wheat that is thrown up against the wind on a high hill, all that will happen is the chaff will blow away, and the real stuff will fall to the ground to be gathered into God's barns.

Jesus knows that we will profess to love him and each other and fail miserably, but he is praying for us that our faith in him and each other will not fail us on the other side of our squabbles. He trusts us to handle our fallings and our failings and let them turn us back to him.

He said to Peter, "When you have repented and turned to me

again, strengthen and build up your brothers" (Luke 22:32). *When*, not *if!* Jesus believed the best about his friends and the best about Peter. They would turn around. Peter would turn around. And not only did he trust them to turn around, he trusted them to use their experience afterward to encourage others. That's what love does; it trusts. It always believes good things will come out of bad things.

Jesus knows we will fail, so we have to meet him on the other side of failure. We will fail to trust him and love each other; we will fail to trust others again who have wounded us. God wants to turn our failures into fresh faith. For this we have Jesus! He will spread his ability to love others throughout our lives and tell us how to get on with it.

It may be a matter of our trusting someone who has failed us many times all over again, just like Jesus had to do. Can we, like Jesus, look at the person who has bitterly disappointed us and see that person not as a loser but as a winner? Can we say to ourselves, *"When* she turns around," not *"if"*?

Would you like to pray about it?

> *Lord, I am on the other side of failure. I blew it. You know; you were there! It's hard to love the family—my own as well as yours. But I hear you want me to and that it matters to you. I want the things that matter to you to matter to me, so I give you permission to give me the motivation I need to work for unity and harmony. Give me ideas of how I can make this happen, and help me to do my part. Amen.*

LOVE SEEKS TO TRUST

We need to thoroughly understand what the word *trust* means before we can proceed to trust those who continue to let us down. It may be there are those who have hurt one of our children or disrupted other relationships. We should know what we are shooting for as we work for love and unity.

The word that Paul uses here, *pistuo*, means "to rely on," "to trust," "to depend on." It means to not be cynical or suspicious. We need to speak out of our love and not out of our hurt. Listen to yourself talking about the person who has hurt you. Are you speaking out of your hurt? Do you sound cynical or suspicious? Do you hear yourself saying, "What did he mean by that remark?" Suspicion kills love. Loving trust, on the other hand, gives the other another chance to hurt us all over again. This way love lets the perpetrator know: "I will trust you again."

We get the best picture of what this means when we think of how God is so trustworthy. We can trust that he is always wanting love and unity among us, and he is actively engaged in making it happen. Love doesn't only want unity; it actively tries to make it happen.

God is on our side. He is in our corner. He is active on our behalf, even when he appears to have his hands tied behind his back and his feet shackled. As we begin to build trust where it has been destroyed in a relationship that has gone bad, it may appear we are on our own, but this is not so. We need to hang on to faith when our best efforts seem to be in vain.

Have you ever asked, "God, just whose side are you on?" I have, many times, and we are not the first to pose that question to the Almighty. The psalmist asked the same question: "I envied the proud when I saw them prosper despite their wickedness. They seem to live such a painless life; their bodies are so healthy and strong. They aren't troubled like other people or plagued with problems like everyone else" (Psalm 73:3-5).

Contrasting that to his own life at that moment, David complains, "Was it for nothing that I kept my heart pure and kept myself from doing wrong? All I get is trouble all day long; every morning brings me pain" (Psalm 73:13-14). In other words, "What's the good of my being good? Lord, whose side are you on?"

Yet as David goes to the temple to look for some answers to this universally asked question, he reminds himself that the wicked have their day coming. He decides he can trust God to sort it all out in the end. "But as for me," he says, "how good it is to be near God! I have made the Sovereign Lord my shelter, and I will tell everyone about the wonderful things you do" (Psalm 73:28).

In other words, I am responsible only for my reactions, not for those of the wicked. It could be I will never see some things resolved this side of heaven, but I will live with this end in sight. I can determine to do my part, so I have no regrets that I didn't give it my best shot.

Trusting God to put all wrongs right in our final future helps us to deal with the ills allowed in our present now. It will be all right because God is on our side. It might not feel like it, and it might not look like it, but God is trustworthy! He can be my refuge now and will be my reward later. Meanwhile, I will believe that the person I am at odds with will respond to all the prayers that are being prayed on his or her behalf.

If we reflect the trustworthiness of God in our attitude, those we love who are hurting and struggling with failure and sin may make a beeline for the safe haven of our hearts. We can be a refuge for them. We may even do the same for the people who are close to us but have failed us or hurt us.

LOVE HANGS ON TO HOPE

If trust is betrayed, we need to hang on to hope. It has been said, "You can't be optimistic with misty optics; seeing what will be with the eyes of faith requires clear inner vision."

Helen Keller, a woman who was both blind and deaf, was asked, "What can be worse than a person with no sight?"

She replied, "A person with sight but no vision."

Hope is ridiculously optimistic. It has vision, insight into what should be and what will be one day. It refuses to be intimidated by a relationship that looks like Humpty-Dumpty who sat on a wall, fell off, and lay shattered in little pieces on the ground. It sees things no one else seems to see. It sees a miracle. It sees Humpty-Dumpty mended and sitting on the wall again!

Helen Keller's teacher was ridiculously hopeful when, humanly speaking, there was so little hope at all in the situation. She believed Helen could become a productive human being. She believed it, she got Helen to believe it because she knew God believed it, and she set out to do her part to make it happen.

We need a lot more teachers like that in the church of Jesus Christ. There are many blind and deaf people who need someone to believe them into usefulness. Many Christians just need someone to say to them, "You can do it! Even if you have tried and failed, you can try again. I'm behind you."

Maybe some of you are wrestling with children who, unlike Helen Keller, have all their faculties, have everything going for them, and yet are a real disappointment to you. Will they ever become what you long for them to be in the Lord? Can you lovingly trust them to become the people they were created to be before Satan got his sticky little fingers on them?

This has nothing to do with our personality either. Some of us are more naturally inclined to be hopeful and trusting of other people. Others are more cynical. God's Spirit transcends all our foibles and personality traits. The most negative thinker among us can become optimistic in the Lord. This is what faith, hope, and love do. In the end it depends not on my performance but on God's promises.

Perhaps you are beating yourself up because you feel your kid would have been a better Christian if you had been a better mother. That is not necessarily so.

I was teaching Proverbs 31 to a class of young mothers. I began by explaining that this "bionic Christian lady" who lurks rather accusingly in these pages didn't really exist except in the imagination of the writer, perhaps King Lemuel, writer of the first nine verses of chapter 31. It was, he says, something "that his mother taught him" (Proverbs 31:1).

I asked the young moms how many of them thought this concept too hard to grasp. Most of them were in the tough child-rearing years, when the idea that their children would ever sit down and lovingly write a poem about their wonderful advice blew their minds! It was too much to hope for, even for the most optimistic of parents. Yet parents need to look past their children's present behavior and with biblical hope, trust their kids to come through. Not because they are bionic Christian parents, but because we have a bionic God!

It's all right to dream, and we should. Dream that our kids grow up to love Jesus to distraction and give themselves sacrificially for a lost and broken world. But we can do more than dream. We can instruct them in the ways of God and make sure they are well versed in Scripture. We can determine to give them as many chances to try and fail as it takes. We can certainly explain that we are only models of growth and learning, not models of perfection. We can point them to God, the perfect parent, who trusts them to be all he wants them to be down here.

Agape love moves us to hope for and believe the best about our kids when they are at their worst. God wants us to reckon on the fact that the incorrigible little liar is of great worth and that through prayer and trust "this too shall pass." Love is the will to believe more than the evidence demands.

Who are you worried about? A husband you are trying to forgive and trust again? A friend who has hurt you? A child who looks as though she will never follow the Lord as you long for her to do? A loved one who is an unbeliever and laughs at your faith? A family of siblings who seem to hate each other? A spouse who has told you the love has run out in your marriage and he wants out? Love them with his love. And, of course, for this you need Jesus, but for this you have Jesus!

Not too long ago I was concerned about two of our grandchildren. Instead of panicking and praying about every new problem that arose, I took a step back and began to pray the "bigger thing" for them. I started to pray for them that they would so love the Lord that they would end up either on the mission field making waves for God or being change makers—instruments of change—in the marketplace. I began to thank God in advance for hearing and answering this prayer.

Almost at once I noticed a difference. As I refused to be intimidated by my concerns for them and began to claim God's best, I witnessed a turnaround in their choices, behaviors, and ambitions. I refused to major on the minors, worrying about every little crisis along the way, but turned my prayers to the major things in their fu-

ture. I prayed about the positives and quit praying about the nega-
tives. I loved and trusted them on my knees before God. Try it!

*Lord God of my grandchildren, I am aching for those I love. Turn them around
for your sake. Direct their feet into the path of life. Make of them mighty forces
for your kingdom. Call them into such a vibrant relationship with you that people
will find Christ through them. May they love you more dearly and know you
more nearly, moment by moment and day by daily day. May they love you as
you love them. And may this spiritual renewal in their hearts and lives spill over
into their family and their world. Lord, I trust you to do this new work of grace
in their lives, and I trust them to respond. Lord, I believe in them. I believe the
best about them. I refuse to think about the worst but leave you to take care of
those dark things. Have your own marvelous way in their lives. Thank you,
Lord, in advance for doing this. How I love and praise you for these things that
shall come to pass. I love and trust you, Lord. Amen.*

Hope is overwhelming confidence in the God who can do anything
with anyone at any time in any place. In Greek thought, hope was essential for man's well-being. The Greeks had a myth that Zeus gave
humankind all good things for life and put them in a jar. Curiosity
lifted the lid, and all the good things in the jar escaped back to the
gods. The lid was slammed shut, and hope was trapped. The gods
knew that hope was essential for the well-being of humankind. That's
a nice fable, but they got one thing very right. Hope *is* essential for the
well-being of humankind! "Where there's life there's hope," the saying goes. The converse is also true. Where there's hope there's life.

Hope is something that belongs very particularly to the Christian. The New Testament talks about a "living hope" (1 Peter 1:3,
NIV). Psychologist Sigmund Freud said we needed to look to the
past for hope. So everyone began to dig up their past. Then came
the people who said, "No, hope is to be found not in the past but in
the present." Then existentialism ruled the day. Now with people's
hearts failing them for fear because of international situations, many
are looking toward the future, trying to find some hope in these uncertain days. This is where Christians come into their own! Christian love always has hope for the future.

Christians actually have the best of all worlds. We can look back on the past and know we are forgiven; we can cope with the problems of the present because we have hope for the future. This hope enables us to keep an eye on what's ahead while being a blessing to people in our here and now. This living hope enables us to cope with all eventualities and sets us free to love people to faith along the way.

LOVE PERSEVERES ON ALL DAYS

Love always hopes. It can't help itself. Always, not some ways or some days, but always on all days. I had a personal experience of this very thing on—of all days—September 11, 2001. I was on United Flight 929 heading for Chicago and home. As the pilot began to dump fuel into the Atlantic, rudely waking the unsuspecting passengers in the cabin from a snooze, I looked over at my neighbor. We both raised our eyebrows.

"Now then," the captain announced over the intercom, "we have a healthy aircraft."

"Well, that's good!" I said. But the cabin crew was suddenly far too busy for my liking. What were they doing? If the plane was healthy and the weather fine, why were we dumping fuel, and why were we unmistakably hearing the wheels being lowered?

I looked at my watch. We were approximately three and a half hours out of London's Heathrow Airport. My husband had seen me off and stayed to minister in Northern Ireland. We had just completed four wonderful weeks of ministry together in Siberia and Russia.

"All airspace and borders have been closed in and out of the United States," the pilot continued. "We have been informed we have a national emergency on our hands and will be landing in twenty minutes at Gander Airport in Newfoundland. I can't tell you any more until we are on the ground. Crew, prepare the cabin for landing."

That was it! My seat companion was a young heart surgeon.

"I hope we aren't going to need you," I said.

"So do I," he replied with feeling.

"So what do you think?" I asked him after a few stunned moments. He shook his head, puzzled.

"Maybe a nuclear reactor?" he suggested.

"Taliban," I said. Having just been in Russia, the Taliban had featured heavily in the news, and they came readily to mind as we debated what on earth could have caused such drastic measures. We couldn't figure out, though, why all the air space and borders in the United States would have been closed. The Taliban was terrorizing people half a world away.

We, along with thousands of others landing in Gander, Newfoundland (doubling the population), were left wondering and not a little apprehensive! Psalm 139:16 came readily to mind. "All the days ordained for me were written in your book before one of them came to be" (NIV).

"Even September 11, 2001, Lord," I murmured.

All 250 of us on the plane hastily read the emergency landing instructions (the ones we never bother to read) in the pocket in front of us. Then I experienced two distinct feelings.

First, a settled certainty that there was nowhere else in the whole wide world that I should be at that moment other than that airplane seat, firmly buckled into the ordained will of God for me.

Every day, the Bible says. Every day. "Lord, that includes September 11 as surely as it means all my yesterdays and all my tomorrows, doesn't it?"

"Yes," said that still small voice in my soul. I recognized the whisper of his grace.

Second, I felt a heady sense of anticipation for whatever was ahead. Of course, none of us in the skies had an inkling of the size and shape of the horrific events that had unfolded in Washington and Manhattan an hour or so after we were airborne.

But God was good to give me thirty minutes before landing to check my theology and make sure it was securely in place before we were informed of the horrible things that had happened.

What did I believe? That God is in control even when I am not?

Yes! That nothing can happen to his children apart from his will? Yes! That God is good—all the time—even when things are bad? Yes! That I and other Jesus lovers and glory givers on that plane had a colossal advantage over those who had no high tower for their souls to run to, no Good Shepherd to calm their beating hearts, hush their fears, and remind them that if the very worst were to happen, the very best was yet to come? Yes!

You see, I had a living hope!

We were still in our seats on flight 929 twelve hours later. We had to wait for processing by the Canadian authorities before leaving our luggage on the plane and being driven thirty miles to the Salvation Army church in Gambo, Newfoundland (I've always wanted to go to Gambo!). I had reason enough to settle into six days of "God experiences." If I really believed what I said I believed, this would be an unprecedented opportunity to do what Stuart and I had just been training pastors, leaders, and missionaries to do all over Russia. Establish a presence, gain credibility, and speak for Christ in the situation to anyone who will listen.

Well, I had established a presence by getting on my flight at Heathrow. No need to take the risks and undergo the rigors of countless missionaries worldwide who intentionally put themselves in harm's way for the sake of Christ and his kingdom. My "village" or "people group" was composed of two hundred passengers and crew from many different cultures and countries, and I was firmly established among them!

Next, I needed to gain credibility. How? I knew the answer to that one. By my reactions to the situations we found ourselves in and by my loving response to those around me. Immediately I faced my first test.

All meals, except for breakfast and emergency rations, had been eaten, so the crew announced they would wait for four hours before feeding us the food they had left. They needed to be careful as they had no idea how long we would be shut up on the plane.

My mind flew to my purse, where I had a packet of biscuits (read "cookies"). A struggle ensued.

I'll wait till everyone's asleep, I thought, *and then nibble them surreptitiously!* I was immediately horrified at myself! *Well, that's a great way to begin to gain credibility,* I lectured my soul. Any fancy ideas I had had of rising to the occasion for Jesus disappeared!

God helped me to do a little bit better as the days went by. Sleeping on a pew or an army cot gets old after six nights—even though I had the joy of a mattress for three of those nights. Sitting around on church chairs for twelve hours a day or lining up for one of the three phones only to hear the busy signal adds up to a lot of frustration. It was time to take spiritual advantage of the situation and seize the day!

I set about my unexpected task to gain quick access to the hearts and minds of the people God had brought into my life for this short time. How to start?

I prayed—all the time. I smiled—all the time, at everybody! I began touching an arm or a shoulder day by daily day and asking simply, "How are you doing?" From the very first day, people responded. In fact, one girl asked me, "What on earth have you got to smile about?" I told her!

I found myself more excited than I could imagine, with a growing consciousness of the importance of every hour. Most important were the precious meal times at the long Salvation Army tables. "Which people should I sit with, Lord?" I prayed as breakfast, lunch, and dinner came along. Meal after meal, I found God had prepared hearts around me.

We were served by Salvation Army staff, whose mercy gift shouted louder than words to all of us. "We lucked out being here," a passenger commented. "I don't know why they have been so giving and kind to us." I told him!

Some needed a challenge or a provoking thought—others needed assurance or comfort. A small child needed a story or a game of cards. I was stretched as others debated deep and difficult things. I tried to put as many links on the chain of salvation as I could, believing others would add theirs in the days ahead. It turned out to be one of the most challenging, frustrating, self-revealing, exciting, productive, God-shadowed weeks of my life!

I certainly didn't win every argument about the character of God ("How could a good God let this happen?") or the wisdom of God ("Why did he make Lucifer in the first place?"). Neither were there necessarily receptive ears to my biblical perspectives ("This is God's world, and he wants it back."). But I got agreement that we were a thankful planeload of people. Thankful to be alive and safe. We had a wonderful captain and crew and lots of passengers who rose to the occasion to keep our spirits up or calm things down when people's patience frayed. We even had a musician, who had been heading to Nashville, sing for us (and with us) for six days. I discovered that the best, and worst, of people comes out in such times.

But I was also thankful for the chance to put some of the faith I talk and write about so easily to work in a difficult setting.

I thought a lot about the prayer I had requested from the pulpit of our church on the eve of this trip to England, Siberia, Russia, and—as it turned out—Newfoundland! I had asked especially for prayers for safe travel.

We had learned that the previous month, the same flight into Irkutsk had crashed, killing all on board. The captain could not get landing permission from the drunken traffic controller, and after the plane had circled the airport for a while, it ran out of fuel. I thought about the four-hour trip on Soviet roads that should have been easy but took twelve hours with many adventures along the way.

I had no doubt whatsoever that our loving friends and family had done sterling battle on their knees—for the devil, as we know, is a murderer from the beginning.

As we recover from the incredible events of September 11 and regroup spiritually for what is around the corner of tomorrow, I am encouraged by my own small experience. God waits with our future in his hands, and it will be all right.

Whatever the whatever, and whenever the whenever, God is God enough! Sadder and wiser, may we Americans return to our God and give ourselves with greater urgency to the most important and necessary things in life. Jesus said, "All of us must quickly carry out the tasks assigned us by the one who sent me, because there is little time left before the night falls and all work comes to an end" (John 9:4). The sun is still in the sky, but perhaps it is setting. We must "carry out the tasks assigned us."

This world in its present form is passing away. In the letter to the Hebrews we read God's promise: "Once again I will shake not only the earth but the heavens also" (Hebrews 12:26). The words "once again" indicate the removing of what can be shaken—that is, created things—so that what cannot be shaken may remain.

Verse 28 says, "Since we are receiving a kingdom that cannot be destroyed, let us be thankful and please God by worshiping him with holy fear and awe." So let's be thankful and worship God.

Hope for tomorrow sets us free for life today—even when there is reason for our hearts to fail for fear—if we love God first, others second, and our selfish selves last. For this we need Jesus!

LOVE ENDURES FOREVER!

Hope for Christians means that we are sure as we face the future. Paul says in Romans 5:5, "Hope does not disappoint us, because God has poured out his love into our hearts by the Holy Spirit, whom he has given us" (NIV).

A spouse may disappoint us, a child may disappoint us, an employee may disappoint us, or a church leader may disappoint us, but God will never disappoint us. We can have New Testament hope—overwhelming confidence—that God will be God at the end of the day. Love stimulates certainty of Christian hope.

Paul says that love believes all things, trusts all things, hopes all things, and endures all things. Hope looks to the final victory of Jesus Christ that Scripture promises. Love endures to the end.

Yet endurance does not set due dates. Endurance is the power to keep hoping without an end in sight. Despair comes from deadlines set too early and hope defined too narrowly. Love always endures.

What happens if after all the believing and all the trusting and all the hoping, the ones we pray for still fail? We hang in there anyway. We endure to the end. We say, "Lord, if they never make it, I will. If they never love you, I will. If they never love each other as I long for them to love each other, I will love them all anyway." The word translated "endure" is *hupomeno* and is a military term. The idea is to endure hardship like a good soldier of Jesus Christ.

During the Second World War, the HMS *Eskimo* was torpedoed and literally sliced in half. Half of it sank immediately. The boat had been built in two halves for this very reason, so half a ship came home.

It seemed that all of England was waiting on the dockside to welcome what was left of the HMS *Eskimo!* The surviving half of the ship limped into port with the sailors standing erect and saluting as the national anthem was played.

So shall some of us come home to God. As we live our lives for Jesus, motivated and activated by love, we shall endure to the end because that's what love does. Love never gives up! When we arrive at home port, standing erect and saluting our Commanding Officer, the bands will be playing and the flags will be flying for us. What a royal welcome that will be!

There is a story of a husband and wife who gave their lives for the Lord in a hardship post on the mission field, far from home and family. At the end of their career, with their health broken, they returned on a ship with many other passengers from foreign parts. They had served their mission with distinction and were excited to come home to their reward.

But the messages about the time of their return were lost, and the reception party and their remaining family members mistook the day of their arrival. When the boat drew near the dock, the old couple scanned the waiting crowds eagerly, looking for a familiar face or a mission banner welcoming them home. They watched the red carpet being rolled out for some entertainers who were on board. Still they saw no one they knew.

Now the rest of the passengers were being greeted and feted.

Bands played, fireworks were set off, and flags flew. But not for them.

The old couple, bewildered and hurt, was the last to disembark. Not one person greeted them. There were no medals, and no speeches were made in their honor. There was no reception after a lifetime of service. Overcome with grief, they held each other tightly, trying to make sense of it all.

"What a welcome home," sobbed the wife. The husband, his own heart breaking, put his arms around her, and they stood there together swaying in their disappointment and grief. Then each of them individually heard an unmistakable voice deep in their heart. It said the same thing to both of them as clear as a bell, as only the still small voice of God can.

You're not home yet!

They looked at each other with joy dawning. "Did you hear it?" they asked each other. And then they both were crying tears of gratitude. There would be another journey on another day, not too far in the future, when they would steam into port looking like HMS *Eskimo!* Half their lives blown away on the mission field for the love of Jesus, and that would be all right. They would be truly home! This then would be their exceeding and great reward.

Love always hopes, always perseveres. Love never fails. Do you need to learn to love and trust again? Look to God who alone can give you that love. For this you need Jesus. For this you have Jesus.

MAKING IT MINE

These questions can be used for personal quiet time or adapted for group discussions. A notebook, a Bible, and a pencil would be useful.

Thinking It Over

1. Do you find it hard to trust someone twice? What has helped you to give people a second chance?
2. Read Luke 22:31-32. Discuss Jesus' treatment of Peter.
3. Discuss or write a sentence about the following statements: Love is overwhelmingly optimistic. Love is the will to believe more than the evidence demands.
4. Share an experience where you were forced to revisit your theology and find out if you really believe what you say you believe.

Praying It In

1. Spend a few moments praying for love and unity in your family.
2. Pray for someone who has broken your trust.
3. Pray for someone who is causing disunity in your family or church (no names if you're praying in a group).
4. Pray for a teenager you know who is giving his or her parents difficulty (again, no names in a group).

Living It Out

1. Think of someone who is terminally ill, and plan to visit that person to share the gospel and the hope of heaven.
2. Using a concordance, look up some verses about heaven and collect the data. Make a list. Share what you learn with someone.

CHAPTER EIGHT

LOVING GOD UP CLOSE
AND PERSONAL

Now we see but a poor reflection as in a mirror;
then we shall see face to face.
1 CORINTHIANS 13:12 (NIV)

IS IT POSSIBLE TO SEE GOD FACE-TO-FACE? OBVIOUSLY PAUL believed that to be true. He told us that even though we don't see everything very clearly right now, one day all will be made clear and we shall see God face-to-face.

That makes me wonder. Remember when Moses asked to see God's glorious presence? God told him, "You may not look directly at my face, for no one may see me and live" (Exodus 33:20). But God said he would make his goodness pass in front of Moses. "As my glorious presence passes by, I will put you in the cleft of the rock and cover you with my hand until I have passed" (v. 22).

Yet earlier in that same chapter, the Bible tells us that "inside the Tent of Meeting, the Lord would speak to Moses face to face, as a man speaks to his friend" (v. 11). Do we have a contradiction here? I don't think so.

When the word *face* is applied to God, it often refers to God's presence (as in Genesis 4:16). It is not that God has a face like you and I. The human face is the part of our anatomy that we use to convey our feelings. God transcends the merely human, but it helps us to use anthropomorphisms (interpretations of what is not human in terms of human characteristics). Moses was allowed to speak with God face-to-face, but he was not permitted to see God's face lest he die. To see God face-to-face is reserved for believers in the life to come!

What an incredible thought it is! You and I will have that privilege when Jesus comes or when he calls for us at our deaths—a privilege that even Moses was denied while here on earth. We will know and see the very presence of God, "the brightness of the glory of God that is seen in the face of Jesus Christ" (2 Corinthians 4:6).

The apostle John, exiled on the island of Patmos because of his faith and his preaching, had a vision of Jesus risen from the dead. He describes the glorified Jesus using inadequate human words because that is all he had to use.

John was "worshiping in the Spirit" (Revelation 1:10) when he heard a voice behind him. He turned and saw the living glorified Christ! Remember, John had spent three years with Jesus. He had seen a glimpse of his glory on the Mount of Transfiguration, but now he looked into the face of his best friend and hardly recognized him. John says, "His head and his hair were white like wool. . . . And his eyes were bright like flames of fire. . . . His face was as bright as the sun in all its brilliance" (Revelation 1:14, 16). John had leaned against Christ's shoulder at the Last Supper and looked into his face, but what he saw at that moment put him on his face! "When I saw him, I fell at his feet as dead" (Revelation 1:17).

John was overcome with the vision, but Christ placed his "right hand" (a symbol of authority and strength) on him and said, "Don't be afraid! I am the First and the Last. I am the living one who died. Look, I am alive forever and ever! And I hold the keys of death and the grave" (Revelation 1:17-18).

When we are in heaven, we shall fall at his feet when we see his face. But he will, without a doubt, put out his right hand and strengthen us to stand in his holy presence. And what is more, he will enable us to look into his face!

You know how it is impossible to look at the sun shining in its strength, even when wearing dark glasses. "For now we see through a glass, darkly" (1 Corinthians 13:12, KJV). But in heaven we will be able, through his enabling, to gaze at his brilliance without fainting.

FACE-TO-FACE

So the best is yet to come! But in his grace, God gives us little previews along the way. But "now we see but a poor reflection as in a mirror; then we shall see face to face. Now I know in part; then I shall know fully, even as I am fully known" (I Corinthians 13:12, NIV). Mirrors were made in Corinth. In fact, Corinth was famous for some of the most beautiful bronze mirrors in antiquity. In those days mirrors consisted of a metal surface made of copper, silver, gold, electrum, or bronze. You can imagine how imperfect the image must have been, no matter how beautiful and polished the surface. Paul contrasts the imperfect image in one of those mirrors with seeing a person face-to-face.

The idea is to become as like Christ as it is possible down here but to allow the future appointment with God to motivate our behavior and give us hope. So how are we doing when we look in the mirror? When we get discouraged about ourselves and our spiritual progress, we can think a little bit about the fact that one day we will really understand ourselves. I will understand myself as God understands me. And one day I will even like myself! I will be like Christ! Do you have a hard time liking yourself? Well, one day there will be a lot to like and accept. One day.

John tells us that when we see Jesus face-to-face, "we shall be like him, for we shall see him as he is" (I John 3:2, NIV). So full knowledge of ourselves will come only when we see Jesus and know him as perfectly as he now knows us. Full knowledge of him will not be ours until that day. Now we live with the imperfect, but one day the perfect reality will be ours. So long as we have not seen Jesus as he is, we are not fully mature.

THE HOPE OF GLORY

Even life lived with a new nature is spoiled by imperfection. But one day everything will be changed, and perfection will come. This is our hope. Hope is confidence that life is worth living in the midst of our present problems because the best is yet to come!

Paul uses the words *now* and *then*. He writes, "*Now* we see but a poor reflection; . . . *then* we shall see face to face. *Now* I know in part; *then* I shall know fully" (I Corinthians 13:12, NIV, emphasis mine). For Paul, *now* is now with all its fallen aspects; *then* will be then, free from all the fallenness of life. We live in a temporary environment in a spoiled creation. We live in the *now* with a view to the *then*.

So we must not be so heavenly-minded that we are no earthly use, but having said that, we are to also "wait for [look for, expect] the blessed hope—the glorious appearing of our great God and Savior, Jesus Christ" (Titus 2:13, NIV). This is the hope that will keep us keeping on! We need to "see" it by faith and allow the truth of his coming and what is ahead to encourage us in the dark times.

The best hope of all will be the advent of Jesus or our call at death. And the incredible experience of seeing him right there in front of us clearly (not in a glass darkly) and ourselves like him . . . Oh, the joy! That is why Paul says:

> Therefore, since we have been justified through faith, we have peace with God through our Lord Jesus Christ, through whom we have gained access by faith into this grace in which we now stand. And we rejoice in the hope of the glory of God. . . . And hope does not disappoint us, because God has poured out his love into our hearts by the Holy Spirit, whom he has given us. (Romans 5:1-2, 5, NIV)

Hope will no longer be necessary in heaven because at that time our hope will be fully realized. Knowledge, imperfect now, will also pass away in total realization and understanding. We could never experience its completeness down here.

Our living hope is the Christ that lives within us. He is the basis of our hope: "Christ in you, the hope of glory" (Colossians 1:27, NIV).

> *The "now" will be brought to an end with the "then,"*
> *Our hope will be realized when he comes again.*
> *He'll come for his own, the redeemed of the race,*
> *With the light and the love of the Lord on his face.*
>
> *The "now" will be "then," when the "then" will be "now,"*
> *Jesus is coming we don't know just how.*
> *But he said it and meant it, he'll come for us all,*
> *And we'll see him and know him, the true light of all.*

Oh, "now" will be "then," and the tears that we shed
And the pain that we knew in the land of the dead
Will be all wiped away by his nail-pierced hand,
And we'll know as we're known in Emmanuel's land.

His glory will fill up the universe small,
Glory of Glory, the true light of all.
Jesus, oh Jesus, the Father's great prize.
The love of his life and the light of his eyes.

When "now" turns to "when," I will revel in him,
Who came to our "now" to forgive all our sin.
Then we'll meet and adore him at his mercy seat,
When we all see his face, and we fall at his feet.

—Jill Briscoe

When living in the "now" gets to be too much to bear, glance heavenward and think of the "then" for a little. Encourage yourself. That's what hope is for!

WATCHING FOR JESUS

So when will the "then" be "now" for you and me? For some of us, it will be at the Second Coming; for others it will be at death. Till our then, we should be on tiptoe, our souls leaning forward in breathless expectation while our bodies busy themselves with kingdom work.

If Paul had a desire to "depart and be with Christ, which is better by far" (Philippians 1:23, NIV), then we, too, should have a desire to look into those things that come after death.

When my father died, a dear clergyman sent me a little poem that was very comforting to me:

Better to be a lark on high,
Singing for joy 'gainst a cloudless sky.
Better to know no sorrow or pain
No darkness or death
But to live again.

Better to breathe in heaven's pure air,
A lamb that is safe in the Shepherd's care
Better far better with Christ to be
Living and loved through eternity.

—R. E. Cleeve

I love that thought, "Living and loved through eternity." Some of us have been shortchanged in this life. We have not been loved. We have not even been liked. Some of us have even been hated. One day we shall be living and loved through eternity. Then we shall not only be loved but be able to love back even as we are loved! We will be able to give love truly and purely and fully for the first time. What will that be like?

Well, we will be eternally patient with everybody! We will be infinitely kind. We will be totally content and so never want for anything. We will only speak sweet and up-building words. And we will understand and experience God's love, in all its depth, breadth, length, and height! We will enjoy endless, persevering love that never fades. We will love God with all our hearts, minds, souls, and strength, and our neighbor as ourselves. And we will experience a love in return that will not consume us but energize us with a love that never ends.

I heard the testimony of a student who was in a Christian college. He and his fellow students were playing a concert for some severely handicapped children in a home run by Christian people. The young people in the band were tired with their tour and grumbled about playing this extra concert, especially as they reckoned the children would not appreciate the fine points of their performance.

They went and played. Afterward the people running the institution asked if they could give them a tour of the home. Again the students sighed and grumbled. However, they complied.

The director of the home asked if John and Butch, two eleven-year-olds, could sing for them. There were more deep sighs and groans. But what could they say? They felt guilty as they had been uncomfortably aware that their concert for the children had lacked heart. They just wanted to get out of there! John and Butch dutifully performed for them. They stood at a microphone and sang,

> *It will be worth it all when we see Jesus;*
> *Life's trials will seem so small when we see Christ.*
> *One glimpse of his dear face all sorrow will erase;*
> *So bravely run the race till we see Christ!*

In the words of that student (now a professor in a Bible school), "I don't know what key [they] sang in. I think it changed several times. From a musical standpoint there were a lot of misplaced notes. But what was missing when we, the musicians, played for them was present when [those boys] sang that song to us!"

Afterward, Butch and John showed the chagrined students around their home. They took them to a large playroom where the kids were having fun. The thing that struck the young men and women most, however, was a huge glass window in the room. The rest of the home was spotless, but this window was smudged and dirty with drool marks all over it.

The director had caught up with the party and said, "Oh, I know what you are thinking. Why don't we clean the window? Well, we actually do clean the window several times a day. The problem is that once the children are done with all their chores, they get free time to come and play in the playroom. The first thing the children do is go up to the big picture window and press their faces against it. Then they look up into the sky to see if Jesus is coming now!"

The professor paused as he told us this story. Years after this experience, the retelling of it still moved him deeply. It moved us, too. Here we all were in our bodies that are perfectly formed with minds that are sharp and capable. Yet all too often we are so occupied with what we can do in our healthy bodies that we forget that Jesus could come back at any time. The professor concluded his message by saying, "We don't have to make a big deal of it. Just glance up several times a day to see if Jesus is coming. It will keep our ministry feet to the fire."

Every Knee Shall Bow

When Jesus comes again, the Bible tells us he will set up his seat of judgment. Whether we have already died or are still alive when he returns, all will stand at the judgment seat of Christ to give an account of the life we have lived down here. Sometimes someone will ask, "Will Christians be judged if they have accepted Christ?" Yes. Paul says to the Christians at Rome, "Remember, each of us will stand personally before the judgment seat of God. . . . Yes, each of us will have to give a personal account to God" (Romans 14:10-12).

Years ago someone gave me a poem that has haunted me a little bit ever since.

When I stand at the judgment seat of Christ
And he shows me his plan for me
The plan of my life as it might have been
Had he had his way, and I see
How I blocked him here and I checked him there
And I would not yield my will,
Shall I see grief in my Savior's eyes,
Grief though I love him still?

He would have me rich, and I stand there poor,
Stripped of all but his grace,
While memory runs like a hunted thing
Down the paths I can't retrace.
Then my desolate heart will well nigh break
With tears that I cannot shed.
I will cover my face with my empty hands
And bow my uncrowned head.
Lord, of the years that are left to me
I yield them to thy hand.
Take me, mold me, make me,
To the pattern Thou hast planned.

—Anonymous

I want to be able to look in his face and not have to "bow my uncrowned head" and look at the floor. I don't want to bow my head in shame but bow my knees in adoration! The Bible tells us that one day, "at the name of Jesus every knee will bow, in heaven and on earth and under the earth, and every tongue will confess that Jesus Christ is Lord, to the glory of God the Father" (Philippians 2:10-11).

When Jesus comes, will we be ready for him?

FIGHTING THE BATTLE

Since we will have to give an account for what we have done, what are we going to say? What will we say about how we have loved?

You see, there is a war going on! And as I Corinthians 13 reminds me, it is not only the war between good and evil but also the war between the selfishness of the fallen human race and the agape love of God that knows no selfishness at all. And we are right in the thick of it!

In T. H. Darlow's words:

> In the everlasting war between love and selfishness Christ calls us to fight on his side. He does not promise us easy service, or sumptuous rations, or wealthy pay; but he makes us understand that to fight this battle is the finest and noblest and most glorious thing in the world—the one thing worth living for. To refuse this call is to miss the very prize and crown of life.
>
> After Napoleon's most amazing victory in Italy, he caused a medal to be struck for his soldiers who fought and conquered in that wonderful conflict. On the reverse of the medal was the name "Marengo" and three proud words, "I was there." (*At Home in the Bible* [New York: G. H. Doran, 1923], 261)

Will I be there? Am I concerned about winning the war? Will I apply myself to win the medal that says, "I was there"? Or will I go AWOL because the battle was too great for me? In this battle, says Darlow, Christ calls us to fight on his side. This is the one thing worth living for!

Jesus says, in essence, "See how much I can make you like me before you walk through my front door." I am at an age in life where I have begun to seriously take stock of my life and decide which battles I am going to fight. There are many battles to fight, but this battle against self is the most important one. If all that will last is love, then love should be my goal.

"There are three things that will endure—faith, hope, and love—and the greatest of these is love" (1 Corinthians 13:13). So I must make love my aim. Will I be able to look God in the eye one day and say, "I was there"? I was there battling away to be more loving than hateful, more patient than angry. I do not want to bow my head in shame and say, "I was not there because I was busy getting my own way."

LOVING WHILE WE'RE WAITING

While we're watching for Jesus, we need to be fighting the battle against self. We need to be loving while we're waiting for his glorious return. We long to see Jesus, but, you see, we *have* seen Jesus!

You may say, "But I live not in the far-off heaven but in the here and now. So what do I do while I'm waiting? How can I glimpse a little of his glory so that I am spurred on till the end?"

It was Philip who said to the Lord, "'Show us the Father and that will be enough for us.' Jesus answered, 'Don't you know me, Philip, even after I have been among you such a long time?'" (John 14:8-9, NIV). In other words, "Look at me, Philip! You are looking at the Father when you look at me!"

When we "look" at Jesus in the Scriptures, we "see" him. This is what we can do while we are waiting. We can learn to love as he loved. We can read the Gospels and see him heal a leper or feed the five thousand. We can hear him teach the Beatitudes or speak words of kindness to sinners. We can watch him in Gethsemane praying for strength to die for us and then breathing his last on the cross—but all this is in our mind's eye. One day we will see him in truth and reality!

After Jesus had risen from the dead, he appeared to the disciples. He said to Thomas, who had been doubting his resurrection from the dead, "You believe because you have seen me. Blessed are those who haven't seen me and believe anyway" (John 20:29).

We have not had a Philip chance or a Thomas chance to see Jesus in reality. But we are happy indeed if we believe in him. One day we shall see him face-to-face.

Meanwhile, we can get to know him by looking at him in the Scriptures. Even a man like Moses, who was privileged to get as up close and personal to God as most of us who have ever lived on this earth, would have to wait for heaven to see completely and not partially. So until then, we enjoy the living presence of the Holy Spirit in our hearts. Our waiting time is to be a busy time!

As we nurture our relationship with God by enjoying his immediate presence by his Spirit, we will find ourselves energized to finish our course with joy. We are left in the world for a reason till that day. There is a war to be won. There are people who need the gospel. There are enemies of Jesus who must be overcome. And, of course, there is the battle that rages not only without but within to be like Christ.

I don't know about you, but I want to be able to look him in the face on that day! I don't want to be ashamed to meet his eye. I hear so many people talking about the fact that they can't wait till Jesus comes and takes us all out of here. That is a rather selfish point of view and perhaps a shortsighted one. He is going to ask us to account for the time we spent here while we were waiting for his return. How did we fight the battle? Were we active in his service until the very last day? We don't want to be so heavenly-minded that we are no earthly use. Above all, how did we love?

HOW'S YOUR LOVE LIFE?

I have to ask myself some hard questions. As I take stock of my "love life," what do I find? Am I more patient than I was when I was a young mother battling the odds against raising and keeping my kids Christian in a non-Christian world? Am I better at responding to suffering? How am I doing with pride? Do I enjoy too much the small acclaim I receive as a Christian writer and speaker? Has it gone to my head? How do I do with dissension? Am I a peacemaker or a warmonger? Am I seeking those I have offended and trying to make amends? And what do I want that I don't have? Have I really come to grips with the constant separation that Stuart and I cope with? After all these years, why do I still struggle with the enemies of resentment, self-pity, and indignation? Just how mature am I? Seeing I am in the autumn, or even the winter, of my life, the time is running out to wage war against my intrinsic selfishness.

Christ calls me to his side. He sounds the battle cry. I hear him say, "Don't give up; go on and grow till I call you home. See how like me I can make you before you walk through my front door!" So how can I pick up my sword and shield and soldier on?

- I can refocus my life on a daily basis. I can determine to talk to him before I talk to anyone else.
- I can thoroughly investigate what it means to meet with him face-to-face. I can take my calendar off the wall and put an appointment with him down day after day, and then show up!
- I can be bold in my asking. I can hold on to him as Jacob did when he wrestled with him, saying, "I will not let you go unless you bless me" (Genesis 32:26).
- I can ask for the outrageous thing—like overcoming fears of things I have no right as a Christian to be afraid of, things that have beaten me all my life. I can say, "No more!"
- I can cling to him until I can honestly say, *Look in my heart, Lord; I trust you! At last, I trust you!* I want to trust him when the battle is at its fiercest. I want to trust him to be all that I need him to be when I need him to be all that I need.
- I can decide to live the latter part of my life with more intensity for Jesus than I have ever lived before.
- I can battle to let all my selfish desires and demands lie at the foot of the cross. For example, my desire that my adult children love each other. The only thing I need to demand is that *I* love my kids. That is enough. I hope that my loving them will cause them to love each other!

- I can talk my head off for Christ and his kingdom, all day long and far into the night. I can decide never to shut up!
- I can write fifty more books, at least! Words are weapons for good or evil. I can determine to use them for Christ and his kingdom.
- I can win the weary war, and the worry war, and the whining war. (Lord, did I hear you say, "It's about time!"?)
- I can search and find the joy in knowing that I do his will every waking moment of every day.
- I can love someone today whom I decided to stop loving yesterday. Yes, I can! And I will! I will love my world in a way I have never loved it before in my life—more patiently and kindly, more sweetly and extravagantly, in more ways than I can count!

All this I can do while I'm waiting. I can do these things because he calls me to do them. He calls me to his side, and one day he wants to hear me say, "I was there!" As I do all these things, I will be becoming more like him. An old Keswick praise hymn puts it this way:

Not I, but Christ, be honored, loved, exalted;
Not I, but Christ, be seen, be known, be heard;
Not I, but Christ, in every look and action;
Not I, but Christ, in every thought and word.

Christ only Christ, no idle word e'er falling;
Christ only Christ, no needless bursting sound;
Christ only Christ, no self-important bearing;
Christ only Christ, no trace of I be found.

Oh, to be saved from myself, dear Lord,
Oh, to be lost in thee;
Oh, that it may be no more I,
But Christ that lives in me.

"Oh, to be saved from myself, dear Lord!" If that is not in your heart, then ask for it. There is no question that I am most like Christ when I am loving, when I am thinking only of others, when I am putting love into action and meeting needs, wiping tears, washing feet, and helping carry people's sorrows and troubles.

> *Not I, but Christ, to gently soothe in sorrow;*
> *Not I, but Christ, to wipe the falling tear;*
> *Not I, but Christ, to lift the weary burden;*
> *Not I, but Christ, to hush away all fear.*
>
> *Not I, but Christ, my every need supplying;*
> *Not I, but Christ, my strength and health to be;*
> *Christ, only Christ, for body, soul, and spirit;*
> *Christ, only Christ; live then thy life in me.*
>
> —*Keswick Praise Hymn Book,*
> Keswick Convention, England

It is as Christ lives his life in and through me that I find I am loving, kind, patient, and humble. He supplies the need. He is my power to be what, in my selfishness, I am not.

LOVE WILL LAST FOREVER

Paul writes, "Love will last forever" (1 Corinthians 13:8) and then says at the end of his magnificent poem of love, "There are three things that will endure—faith, hope, and love—and the greatest of these is love" (v. 13). It follows then, that if love will last forever, and if forever is in heaven, then heaven must be full of a whole lot of love!

So where is heaven? Or rather, *what* is heaven? Remember, we see only through a glass darkly. But we can see some images, though vaguely, in the bronze face of the mirror of time. We have words from the Scripture to help us, even though Paul says, "No eye has seen, no ear has heard, and no mind has imagined what God has prepared for those who love him" (1 Corinthians 2:9).

For most of us, getting to what God has prepared will require us to "walk through the valley of the shadow of death," as the psalmist wrote in Psalm 23:4 (NIV). Death is the last enemy! No one pretends that death itself is a friend. The other side of death is a fine thing, but getting there is a different matter! All of us may be forgiven for dreading the process of dying, but we can endure the pain, looking ahead to the release of the spirit from the body.

Some years ago I was asked to tour a hospital. We began by looking at the gynecological ward. Babies burped and gurgled. It was such a happy place. At the end of the tour, we walked through the hospice unit. How different the atmosphere. "I see this is your birthing wing," I observed to my guide.

The hospital official smiled indulgently. "No, no, this is the hospice. We began in the birthing wing!"

"I beg to differ," I replied. "This is the birthing wing! Here the spirit struggles to be born into the afterlife, as surely as the baby struggles to be born into this life." The official gave me a strange look, but it led to an interesting conversation with a tour member.

So what happens when we are "birthed" into heaven? What will it be like? What shall we see?

There will be light—brilliant, glorious light emanating from the Lamb that will light the home of God. "The city has no need of sun or moon, for the glory of God illuminates the city, and the Lamb is its light" (Revelation 21:23).

Heaven, though glorious, will dim in comparison to him who will shine like the sun in its strength! We shall fall at his feet and cry,

Thou shinest, and all other lights flee,
How could they stay within the bright beam of thy grace.
Your glory fills eternity, No corner lighter than another!
　　　　　　　　　　　　　—E. T. London, 1933

So there will be no more night. And there will be no Office of Homeland Security! The Bible goes on, "Its gates never close at the end of day because there is no night" (Revelation 21:25). Because there is such light and no dark corners in heaven, there will be no dark and secret deeds done. In fact, there will be no wrongdoing at all, forever! This will be a city where righteousness lives.

Because there is light forever, there will also be life forever. Flowers will never fade; leaves will never turn brown. There will be no more death. Every time I go to a funeral, I think, *One day I will never have to do this again!* There will be no need of medicine because no one will ever get sick. And there will be no more pain. Oh, won't that be a day to look forward to? Life, eternal life, will take care of all these things!

There will be no more tears, for "God will wipe away all their tears" (Revelation 7:17). What tears are these and how can they be shed in heaven? That is a mystery. Perhaps they will be fresh on our cheeks as we arrive, crying, from the birthing wing into the rarefied air of our new environment. Or maybe they will be tears of sorrow because the family circle is broken and loved ones are not there. Whatever those tears are about, God will wipe them away forever. In heaven "he will remove all of their sorrows, and there will be no more death or sorrow or crying or pain. For the old world and its evils are gone forever" (Revelation 21:4).

In heaven there will be love that lasts. For how long? Beyond eternity. Paul wrote that love lasts forever. Above all things, there will be love! For God is love, and heaven is his domain. Everlasting Love will wrap his eternal arms around us, and so we shall be loved forever!

So in the light of all of this, the most important thing that should totally absorb our lives down here is the practice of real love. Why? Because love lasts. Love will be the only thing that matters in all eternity!

MAKING IT MINE
These questions can be used for personal quiet time or adapted for group discussions. A notebook, a Bible, and a pencil would be useful.

Thinking It Over
1. Think about or discuss the chapter title, "Loving God Up Close and Personal." What does this say to you?
2. Read Exodus 33:11 and 33:20. Do you see a contradiction? How do you resolve it?
3. Read Revelation 1:9-19. What did God intend to be the result of the vision he gave to John? (See verse 19.) What application can you draw from this?
4. What is the war against selfishness all about?
5. Read the poem about the "now" and the "then." What did you like and why?
6. Think about or discuss the idea of the "birthing wing."
7. Which of the aspects of heaven do you get excited about and why?
8. Has this chapter taken away any fear of death you might have had? Which aspect?

Praying It In
1. Pray for people you know who are frightened about dying.
2. Pray that your minister will make the gospel clear in preaching.
3. Pray for places in the world that know nothing of these things. Pray for people to tell them.
4. Pray for peace in our time so there will be a free world to respond to kingdom workers.

Living It Out
1. Make your own action list of twelve things you intend to do in light of this study.
2. Make absolutely sure of your own salvation.
3. Write a letter to God about this commitment, and keep it in your Bible.

Epilogue

For those of you who like to borrow words because words don't come easily, I suggest you pray the poem prayer below. This is a prayer I penned one Easter at a low point in my life. As I celebrated in my soul all that Jesus had done for me, I was able to refocus on the blessed hope I have in Christ. By the end of my prayer, all was well with my soul again. I invite you to share my prayer, and I trust it will set your soul singing as it did mine. God bless you.

In your presence, Lord, there is hope. May even the hopeless among us believe again. Lord, in your presence there is love. May the most bereft of love discover all that they need. Lord, in your presence there is health in every dimension. Breathe on us, Breath of Life.

> *Love us back to health and wholeness,*
> *Warm us from our spirit's coldness,*
> *Fire us up with grace and glory,*
> *Help us tell your wondrous story.*
> *Jesus, we're your lifeboats ready,*
> *Keep us going, keep us steady.*
> *Save the shipwrecked souls a-sinking,*
> *Save them from their fruitless thinking.*
>
> *Praying, going, reaping, sowing,*
> *Teaching, training, knowledge gaining.*
> *Show us how to serve our brothers,*
> *Those inside the church and others.*
> *Stretch us, grow us, Lord, flow through us,*

Keep us faithful, giving, grateful,
Help us die to self and selfness,
Telling worlds about your greatness.

Lord, we're little, fragile, brittle,
Gently break us, then remake us,
Jesus, lover, friend, and brother,
How we want to love each other.
Fill us, grace us, sternly face us,
With our weakness teach us meekness.
Chide us, feed us, lead us, guide us,
Melt us, make us just like Jesus. Amen!

Other Books by Jill Briscoe

Daily Study Bible for Women
One Year Book of Devotions for Women
Prayer That Works
Faith Enough to Finish

About the Author

Jill Briscoe's active speaking and writing ministry has taken her to many countries. She is the author (or coauthor) of more than forty books, including devotional material, poetry, study guides, and children's books. Jill is the executive director of *Just Between Us,* a magazine providing encouragement to ministry wives and women in leadership. She also serves on the board of directors for World Relief and for Christianity Today International.

A native of Liverpool, England, Jill began working in youth evangelism after becoming a Christian at age eighteen. She and her husband, Stuart, were married in 1958, and since that time they have ministered together through Telling the Truth media ministries at conferences and missions organizations around the world.

Jill and Stuart live in suburban Milwaukee, Wisconsin, where Stuart ministered for thirty years as senior pastor of Elmbrook Church. Both Stuart and Jill now serve as ministers-at-large. They have three grown children, David, Judy, and Peter, and enjoy the blessing of thirteen grandchildren.

To contact Jill or Stuart Briscoe,
call 1-800-248-7884
or visit **www.tellingthetruth.org**

For more information about *Just Between Us,*
a magazine of encouragement for ministry
wives and women in leadership,
call 1-800-260-3342, or
visit **www.justbetweenus.org**